YOUR IT
CAREER

GET NOTICED, GET PROMOTED, AND BUILD YOUR PROFESSIONAL BRAND

52 Great Career Tips for Techies

by ITworld columnist/blogger
Eric P. Bloom

Copyright © 2012

All rights reserved.

ISBN: 1480205761

ISBN 13: 9781480205765

Library of Congress Control Number: 2012920504
CreateSpace Independent Publishing Platform
North Charleston, South Carolina

To Emily and Jesse

Emily: Even though you will soon be a bride, you'll always be my little girl.

Jesse: Welcome to the family, it's wonderful to have you join us.

Love, Dad

Acknowledgements

Writing a weekly blog/column for ITworld has been much, much more than simply deciding on a weekly topic, writing the prescribed number of words, having it edited, and posting it to the website. This column has been an education for me, I hope of value to others, and the basis for this book.

I would like to begin by thanking my Executive Editor at ITworld, Jodie Naze. Her belief in me allowed my blog to begin, and her support and guidance allowed it to continue and mature. I would also like to thank Jodie for her willingness to write the book's foreword. I'm honored and truly appreciate your efforts; thank you. I would also like to thank John Gallant, the chief content officer for IDG Enterprise, for his confidence in me and for my initial introduction to Jodie and others at ITworld.

Next, I would like to thank my readers, those who e-mailed me questions about their career, and those who spent their time and deep thought making comments on what I had written. The combination of these questions and comments has greatly enhanced my writing, expanded my insights, and enhanced the quality of my blog.

Next, I would like to thank my blog proofreaders, Harold and Barbara Bloom, who week in and week out have carefully read and edited my blogs prior to my posting them on the website. Yes, I'm related to this proofreading duo—they're my parents. Truth be told, not only do they do a great job, but it's also just great to be working them. :)

Lastly, I would like to thank my wife, Cheryl, who has continually and patiently listened to me talk about the blogs, columns, and books I'm writing, even though, she has little or no interest in the actual topics. Thanks, honey.

YOUR IT CAREER
GET NOTICED, GET PROMOTED, AND BUILD YOUR PROFESSIONAL BRAND

Foreword By Jodie Naze xi

Introduction xiii

Enhancing Your Technical Skill Set 1
    Your Technology Skills Have A Two Year Half-Life
    And 6 Ways To Stay Current 5
    Your Technology Skills Have A Two Year
    Half-Life – Part 2 9
    Java Developer Should Learn About Databases..... 13
    Cross Training Can Help You Grow 15
    Cobol Programmer Needs A Job Or New Skills 17
    4 Skill-Based Activities For Techies 19

Enhancing Your Non-Technical Skill Set................ 23
    10 Soft Skills Every Business Analyst Needs 27
    5 Important Presentation Tips For Techies 29
    The Hard Skill – Soft Skill Debate For Techies.... 33
    Embrace Your Dormant Skills And Abilities....... 37

Job Search Tips 41
    How To Find A Job Working Remotely – It's Easier
    Than You Think!............................... 45
    When To Take Old Information Off Your Resume .. 47

10 Innovative Places To Find A Great It Job 49
Entrepreneurship Can Help You Find A Job 53
23 Resume Writing Tips For Techies 57
4 Ways To Combine Web-Based And Face-To-Face-Based Job Hunting For Great Results. 61

In The Work Place 65
10 Great Ways To Start A New It Job On The Right Foot 71
Does Telecommuting Make You Invisible? 75
Motivation: 14 Simple Ways To Motivate Development Teams. 79
Don't Like Your Job, Define One You Like 83
What's On Your Laptop Can Be Career Limiting. . . . 87
It's Ok To Say "No" 91
Overworked? Maximize Your Productivity By Knowing Your Zone 95
6 Ways To Help Manage Your Boss 99
The Top 10 Ways To Be A Bad Technical Manager. . 103

Maximizing Your Pay 105
Can Techies Increase Their Salaries Without Becoming Managers?. 109
Contract Programmer Considers Permanent Employment 113
Can The Job Title Data Scientist Raise Your Pay? . . 115

Managing Your Career. 117
An Mba Or A Masters In Computer Science? It's Your Call. 121
Proactively Manage Your Career 123

    8 Ways A Career Coach Can Help Your Career.... 127
    7 Questions To Ask Yourself When Selecting An
    Industry For Your Next Job...................... 131
    5 Great Jobs And 6 Great Company Startup
    Ideas For People With Search Engine
    Optimization (SEO) Skills...................... 135
    Your Hobbies Can Help Your Career 139
    6 Great Social Media Jobs Within It 141

Career Advancement Tips And Advice................... **145**
    Cloud Computing Can Help Or
    Hurt Your Career............................. 149
    Helpdesk Support Technician Wants More....... 153
    Programmer Seeks Advice On How To Become A
    Manager..................................... 155
    Change Is A Four Letter Word: "Gold" And
    6 Great Ways To Get Some 157
    7 Places To Step Outside Your Comfort Zone
    And Get Promoted 161

Building Your Professional/Technical Brand **165**
    6 Great Social Media Tips For Techies 169
    Value Of Technical Conferences 173
    Value Of It Certifications...................... 177
    Helping Build Open Source Software Can
    Help Your Career 181
    Top 10 Reasons Get A Pmp Certification,
    Even If You're A Seasoned Pro.................. 185
    I Want To Work In A Project Management
    Office (Pmo)................................. 187

- Building Your Personal Brand 189
- **Joining It From Other Professions 193**
  - Great It Jobs For Science And Math Majors...... 195
  - Changing Career From Finance To It............ 199
  - 5 Great It Jobs For English Majors 201
  - 5 Great It Jobs For Artists..................... 203
- **Final Thoughts 207**

Foreword

There's never been a more exciting time to be in IT. New technology trends are creating exciting job opportunities in many industries, and companies openly admit that the hottest, most in-demand skills in a competitive market will cost them. Not to mention, the price for *not* having the appropriate IT resources in place can be significant, if not devastating, to the corporate bottom line.

The explosion of mobile technologies, the consumerization of IT, cloud computing, and big data are just some of the latest trends driving these changes. They're forcing IT to rethink how they work with the business, redefining their role and responsibilities, and are often creating jobs requiring different skill sets. As a result, technology leaders must find skilled professionals to take on these new challenges, or grow the expertise in house.

Are you ready to take advantage of the opportunities that these trends offer? More importantly, have you mapped out goals, and a plan for reaching those goals over the next few years? If not, there's no time like the present.

One thing's for certain: IT professionals come from all walks of life, and the career path is often as unique as the individual. You may be considering a career in IT, or just starting out. You might be building onto an established career, or making a midcourse correction. Or perhaps you're switching to IT from an entirely different career. Whatever the situation, you'll find something in these pages to help you along the way.

This book covers a lot of ground, starting with the hard-core technical skills you need now, and how often you need to update them. Soft, nontechnical skills never go out of vogue, so listening, and communication, teamwork, and problem-solving tips are provided as well. You'll get advice on how to find and get that dream job through smart resume writing and networking. If you already have a job you love, fine-tune your satisfaction by learning when to say no or creatively motivating yourself and your team. Last, and probably most important, is the advice on how important it is to build your professional and technical brand through things like social media, technical conferences, and certifications.

What makes this IT career book different from others is that it's based on years of hard-earned experience. Eric Bloom has walked in just about every IT shoe there is—from developer through the ranks to CIO—and he shares the lessons he's learned along the way. These tips reflect a deep understanding of the challenges IT professionals face at every stage in their career, and they will serve you well through yours.

Jodie Naze
Editor in Chief
ITworld

Introduction

As the title suggests, this book is a compilation of a year's weekly blog posts from my "Your IT Career" blog with www.ITworld.com.

I do have to say it's been a fascinating year.

- A few blogs went viral.
- Questions sent to me by readers expanded my perspective on IT career issues, concerns, and goals.
- Topics I researched for potential blogs widened my knowledge of the IT profession I have been a member of for almost thirty years.
- E-mails and posts from readers around the world have made me truly believe that techies are techies, regardless of their gender, country of origin, or educational level. They all want to learn new skills, be successful in their chosen vocation, and grow professionally.
- I've received e-mails from gen-X-age children asking me advice on how their baby-boomer-age parents can learn new technical skills and from baby-boomer-age parents asking advice on how their gen-X-age children can find technical jobs.

I grew up through the IT professional ranks. I began my professional career programming in COBOL and, I must also admit, a number of other programming languages which are long gone and only vaguely recollected in the minds of aging baby-boomer techies like me. From my original programming roots, I moved up the technical and managerial ranks to various executive IT management positions.

Having made this journey from junior programmer to CIO, I had incorrectly believed that I understood what it was like today for techies new to our profession or for more seasoned techies who had made the decision to stay technical rather than move into IT management ranks. Well, I was wrong for a number of reasons.

- The world of high tech today is very different than when I was a hands-on software developer.
- Being of the baby-boomer generation, I have a different mentality than my younger technical brethren. They grew up at a different time, were shaped by different world events, and are at a different stage of life.
- For my technical contemporaries, that is to say, baby boomers who stayed technical, while I share their age, I no longer share their profession. They are professional technologists, and at this point I'm a professional manager and more recently a trainer and entrepreneur. As an aside, I loved being a full-time techie and miss it in many ways.

All that said, I have learned an enormous amount about the issues, trials, and tribulations facing today's technical professionals. This newfound knowledge, combined with my professional journey and senior IT executive experience, has allowed me to provide career advice to those who read my weekly blog and to you reading this book.

This book, as you know, from the first line of this introduction, is a compilation of fifty-two weeks of weekly columns/blogs formed into chapters by topic, and enhanced by commentary that has been written specifically for this manuscript.

My expectation is that no one reader will find all the topics, tips, and advice to be of value. My hope, however, is that each reader finds a few selected topics that truly provide value as he/she tries to successfully navigate his/her IT career. For some it will simply be the resume-writing advice, for others it will be helping them to define their professional brand, and for others it will be a plethora of other similar but different career-related topics.

My hope for you is that you find value in this book and find at least a few tidbits of knowledge, insight, and/or advice that help you reach your professional aspirations.

Until then, work hard, work smart, and continue to grow.

Best wishes and happy reading,

Eric

ENHANCING YOUR TECHNICAL SKILL SET

The columns contained in this chapter all relate to enhancing your technical skill set. In this context, consider a "skill set" to be knowledge in a specific computer programming language, database, software application, hardware device, data communication device, and operating system, or any other computer-based technology that you have the technical, hands-on ability to provide services for at a professional level.

The first two columns in this chapter are related and based on the premise that if you take the exact skill set and technical knowledge you have today, move into a cave for two years, and learn nothing new technically during that time, then when you exit the cave you will only be half as marketable as you were the day you entered. This is because technology moved forward and you did not.

The reason for this phenomenon is that during your two years of cave dwelling:

- software and hardware vendors announced new releases of their products;
- new industry megatrends, such as cloud computing and mobile devices, have changed he industry landscape; and

- newly announced technologies were introduced and have become the new leading edge within the industry.

On the day the first of these two columns was published in ITworld, it went totally viral. There were thousands and thousands of website hits and hundreds and hundreds of column-related comments within the first few days. The reason is that this topic hit a deep chord within the technical community. It was fascinating to watch.

There was so much commentary on the first column that I wrote a follow-up column to further explain the concept.

The next column, "Java developer should learn about databases," is rather special to me for three reasons. First, it was my first ITworld column, and I must admit that I was very excited to see it online. Second, it was based on a question I have been asked many times throughout my career, and I always had the same response, which you can read within the column. Third, early in my career I asked this same question to someone more experienced than I, and his answer is outlined in this column. By now giving others this advice, I'm saying thank you by paying it forward to the next generation of techies.

The column "Cross training can help you grow" was also one of my earliest columns. It's funny, looking back on earlier columns; I had forgotten that the original length was about three hundred words. Somewhere along the line they expanded from this shorter length to an average length of six hundred to seven hundred. Now back to the topic at hand. This column was inspired by a reader who feared that cross training someone else on the application he supported would increase his risk of termination even though he was also being cross trained to perform someone else's job. Rather than give my answer away here, I'll let you read the column.

The column "COBOL programmer needs a job or new skills" is one of my favorite ITworld stories because I know of two specific people that were helped by this column. The first person was the one who asked me the original question that inspired the column. The second person was the father of one of my readers. Her father, in his fifties, had been a COBOL programmer for his entire career and had been recently laid off. Out of concern for her father, she e-mailed me asking if I would speak with him to discuss his professional options. I agreed. Her father and I spoke by phone and I told him two things. First, we discussed his future career options. Then, before we got off the phone, I told him, parent to parent, that I thought it was wonderful that his daughter was going to such great lengths to help her father find a job. He thanked me for my advice and agreed with me that he was blessed to have such a wonderful daughter.

The last column in this section, "Four skill-based activities for techies," is a story about a techie who loves doing technical work, at work and at play, and also wants to do something good for the world. If you are this type of person, you'll love this column.

Now, enough for my commentary; enjoy the columns.

YOUR TECHNOLOGY SKILLS HAVE A TWO-YEAR HALF-LIFE, AND SIX WAYS TO STAY CURRENT

The question I was asked:

Professionally I customize software modules on a well-known software package. The version we are working on is one version back and about a year old. Is continuing to work on this old software version hurting my professional marketability?

My answer:

The short answer to your question is no, not yet, unless it was a major release that is being quickly and widely adopted.

The longer answer is that, in my opinion, a techie's skill set from a marketability perspective has a two-year half-life. That is to say, the exact set of skills you have today will only be half as marketable two years from now.

The reason your technical marketability degrades so quickly is because technology, like time, marches forward. Software companies continually update their applications. Hardware vendors upgrade their hardware and software control systems on an ongoing basis. Also, technology-oriented megatrends like cloud computing and the proliferation of mobile devices are continually driving and transforming our industry.

Your ability to stay current in your technical niche can be greatly affected by the company where you work. That said, regardless of whether your firm is an early adopter, mainstream adopter, or late adopter of new software versions, there are things that you can do to keep yourself current on the technology, including the following:

If it exists, become involved in the vendor's official user group. This can give you special access to the vendor's employees and help you build a network of other techies using the vendor's technology.

1. If your company has no immediate plan to upgrade the vendor's newest software version, ask your manager if you can load the software upgrade into a test region so you can begin to learn about it for future reference.

2. Many software vendors now have cloud-based versions of their software. That said, as a client, they may be willing to give you a free test area within their cloud environment to evaluate and learn their latest software version.

3. Read all you can about the vendor in general and the release notes and industry commentary on the software package. This will help keep you current on your vendor's plans and technology challenges.

4. Read about technologies that are complementary and/or integrated with your vendor's software. For example, if you work on Oracle's financial software product, stay knowledgeable on software, such as report writers, that can be used to enhance its usability. Additionally, if you are writing database-stored procedures, keep up to date on Oracle's PL/SQL.

5. Read and stay knowledgeable about your vendor's major competitors. For example, once again, if you work on Oracle's financial software package, read about what SAP is doing on their product. This will give you a wider understanding of your application specialty and potentially give you insights into innovative ways to customize your vendor's software within your company.

Until next time, work hard, work smart, and continue to grow.

YOUR TECHNOLOGY SKILLS HAVE A TWO-YEAR HALF-LIFE— PART TWO

Last week's blog, "Your technology skills have a two-year half-life, and six ways to stay current," was heavily read and hotly debated. Thank you to all, and here is my reply.

Thanks for all your e-mails and blog comments on last week's column. I love people's feedback to my columns as it helps me look at things from different points of view. Quite frankly, I agree with almost all that you have written.

To begin, the original question asked by the reader was related to the customization of a software package, rather than programming in a base technology, like C and PHP, which has a different set of factors.

As a software package example, in the late 1980s I was a DBA working on Oracle Version 3. Whereas Oracle is obviously very alive and well, none of the database tools or processes I worked on then still exist. This was pre-PL/SQL, and query optimization had to be done by hand because the SQL engine didn't work all that well. Oracle as a software package then is totally different than Oracle the software package now. Sure, data normalization is the same, but virtually all of my exact Oracle 3.0 skill set at that time is now outdated.

Is the knowledge I had then transferable to the latest version of Oracle now? Yes, I believe it is. But to the original point, my Oracle Version 3 skills were much more marketable in 1988 than they are today. Potential employers looking for a DBA would consider my knowledge to be old, and thus I would be less desirable than someone with more current knowledge.

There were also a number of comments stating that C was very marketable twenty years ago and is still very marketable today. These comments are 100 percent correct. I love programming in C. I was also a C programmer. In fact I wrote a (marginally coherent) book based on the original Brian Kernighan and Dennis Ritchie C. It's a great language. Knowing C made it easier for me to learn Pascal, JavaScript, PHP, and a number of other languages.

Even C, however, evolved into C++. Imagine if today you only know K&R C and didn't understand function overloading, structured programming, base classes, and other related advances, such as ODBC, XML, and multithreading.

Also, C now has more competition than it did then, same as COBOL, which I also programmed professionally. There are fewer companies today programming in C and COBOL because of Java. I'm not saying that Java is better or worse than C or COBOL, I'm just saying that they were used more widely in 1990 than they are today, thus further reducing the marketability of older technologies. If fact, I loved Borland Turbo-C, which of course today is far less marketable than the Microsoft .NET tool set.

I would also like to specifically address a number of comments regarding the faulty thinking of HR professionals and hiring managers who think knowledge of a language like C provides no basis for understanding a language like Java. I also think this logic is faulty. Here are two examples. First, I was a Microsoft ASP programmer. I personally found that being an expert in Microsoft ASP made learning PHP extremely easy. Basically, all I had to learn was the new syntax. Second, I was a C programmer who had to learn Java. I must admit that when trying to learn Java, I had to learn to use Eclipse, it had some funky new inheritance rules I had to learn, and the packaging part took me a little getting used to. But, like ASP to PHP, once I got the basics down, my programming skills were extremely transferable. Hearing these comments, I wonder if these managers were ever C programmers themselves. My thought is they were not.

Lastly, I would like to return to my earlier comment regarding base technology, like C and PHP, having a different set of factors. I think with these base technologies, their marketability half-life can be much more variable than just simply two years, but I think the basic concept is sound. This half-life could be dramatically shorter or longer based on the technology and your timing. For example, if you were an ASP programmer the day Microsoft announced .NET, then this half-life was almost immediate. I know because I lived through it. On the other hand, if you are primarily a PHP or COBOL programmer at a time of relatively low technological enhancement, the half-life would be longer, assuming, of course, that the general demand for your skill set remained constant.

In closing, I would like to specifically thank one of my readers, S. T., who sent me a couple of great e-mails on this topic. Thanks! :-)

Oh, one more thing. A few of the blog comments referred to me as a marketing person. I hope from today's blog you now know I'm a techie.

Best wishes to all, and thanks again for your great commentary. I really appreciate your input.

Until next time, work hard, work smart, and continue to grow.

JAVA DEVELOPER SHOULD LEARN ABOUT DATABASES

The question I was asked:

I'm a Java developer. Is it worthwhile spending the time to expand my database skills beyond basic skills?

My answer:

In a word, yes. As a programmer, it is very advantageous to have strong database skills. It makes you more professionally rounded, more versatile, and, as a result, more marketable.

With the exception of certain specialized application types, the majority of applications are designed to move data in and out of databases. Therefore, your ability to manipulate data increases your software development capabilities.

When I think of database skills, I mentally divide them into three primary skill sets: database design, stored procedure writing, and database production. Database design, as the name suggests, is the ability to analyze the data being stored and construct an appropriate database structure which balances data usage flexibility, data storage efficiency, and application performance. Stored procedures are similar to application software, but written using a database-specific programming language designed to store, manipulate, and retrieve data. Database production is the process of allocating needed disk space, re-indexing overworked indexes, and other ongoing production processes. As a programmer, you would be best served to first learn to program stored procedures and then expand your skills to include database design. Learning database production would be an advantage, but as a programmer, it's not as important as the other two.

There is one more thing to consider regarding database knowledge. Over the years, various front end technologies have come and go, but the data remains. A deep understanding of data storage, data movement, and data usage will be valuable to you throughout your professional career.

Until next time, work hard, work smart, and continue to grow.

CROSS TRAINING CAN HELP YOU GROW

The question I was asked:

My manager wants another .NET programmer and me to cross train each other on the applications we support. Does this put my job at risk?

My answer:

My belief is that cross training will not put your job at risk. If your manager wants to get rid of you, he/she will find a way regardless of cross-training-related activities. From an IT manager's perspective, it's very uncomfortable to only have one programmer who knows how to maintain a specific application. Cross training is an ideal way to remedy this issue. This is particularly true if the software is part of an important company process. The issue for your manager is that if you (or the person whose application you are learning) cannot be reached, goes on vacation, changes jobs, or leaves the company, then there is no one that can fix the software. This will make the manager look ineffective and raise issues regarding his/her ability to manage.

This cross training may be a big win for you for a number of reasons.

- First, having another programmer who can support your application will make it easier for you to take vacation, get assigned to a new, exciting project, or even get promoted.

- Second, by being cross trained on the other person's project, you will be expanding your knowledge and versatility, thus increasing your value to the company.
- Third, by explaining your software to another person, you and/or the person you are training may think of ideas for future enhancement or find places in the code that need improvement.
- Next, by being trained in the other application, you may learn some interesting programming tricks that you can add to your programming repertoire.

Lastly, after being cross trained, you will have the ability to maintain both software applications. This makes you more valuable to your manager because you can perform more tasks within the department.

Until next time, work hard, work smart, and continue to grow.

COBOL PROGRAMMER NEEDS A JOB OR NEW SKILLS

The question I was asked:

I'm a COBOL programmer with about thirty years of experience and have been out of work for just over two years. Is it too late for me to learn new marketable skills? If not, what should I learn?

My answer:

Let me begin by asking you two questions. First, what do you like to do and want to learn? Second, how can you pivot your current credentials and knowledge into a new job?

Before discussing the above questions, know that COBOL is still alive and well and living in many large companies within the United States and abroad. You can find these companies by looking for firms that had large COBOL programming staffs in the 1960s, 1970s, and 1980s. Many of the very large and very impressive systems that were developed at that time are still in production today and almost impossible to replace. Additionally, the older baby boomers that built and have been maintaining these systems are retiring in higher numbers, but the systems still remain. If you can find these companies, you very possibly will find employment. On a personal note, I was a COBOL programmer once and loved it.

Now, regarding my two questions above. Your answers to these questions can help you decide what to do next. The trick to quickly changing your professional direction is how effectively you can use your prior work experience to catapult you into a new role. This, of course, raises a third question: what types of applications did you develop as a COBOL programmer? For example, if you spent thirty years developing accounting-related applications such as accounts receivable and payable systems, you could try to pivot this experience into a business analysis role related to those types of systems. Based on your interest and experience, other potential nonprogramming positions that would keep you in a large system environment include disaster recovery planning, capacity planning, and database management.

If you would prefer to stay technical, certainly Java and .NET come to mind, but if you take this path, understand that there will be a large learning curve because these technologies have a very different orientation than COBOL.

I was originally a COBOL programmer and eventually moved to programming in C. I had thought a programming language is a programming language, and if I could do one well I could use any language well. I did eventually become a very strong C programmer, but the transition was much harder than I anticipated because of differences in variable scope, program structure, general development environment, terminology, and other related items.

Another potential technology to consider if you have done a lot of relational database work is learning/expanding your knowledge in database stored procedures, such as Oracle PL/SQL or other similar technology.

Until next time, work hard, work smart, and continue to grow.

FOUR SKILL-BASED ACTIVITIES FOR TECHIES

The question I was asked:

I'm the technology person at a small training company and take care of all things techie (hardware, software, data communication, etc.). Can you suggest any things I could do in my free time that are fun, a little bit techie, would help me at work, and will help people?

My answer:

Wow, what a great question. My assumption, by the way you worded it is that you want suggestions that will meet all four of your criteria. Truth be told, I decided to answer this question in my column for two reasons; first, it really made me think, and second, I have a training business that's heavily tech oriented.

OK, here I go. I can't promise that each one of my suggestions will meet all four of your needs, but I can comfortably say that each option will at least meet three of the four.

Play instructional-based videos (fun, techie, and will help at work)

Game-based learning is an up-and-coming trend in the training world. When playing these games, consider:

- the overall structure of the game to see how it creates a learning environment;
- the techniques used to deliver the training materials;
- the use of graphics and voiceovers;
- the way this technology could be used to deliver your company's training materials.

The key takeaway here is that you should learn more about your industry in general and the technologies that are used by your firm's competitors. This knowledge can make you more valuable to your company and move you toward being the internal go-to person regarding information on technical innovations within your industry.

Volunteer to be the tech person for a nonprofit, charitable, religious, or issue-based organization that you believe in (fun, techie, will help at work, good for the world)

Organizations of this type generally appreciate the involvement of technically oriented people to help with their website, e-mail blasts, and other communication-related technologies. Helping out within these organizations can be fun, because I have found that the people associated with these types of organizations are generally fun to be with, committed to doing good for the world, and personally inspiring. Regarding helping you at work, it can give you the chance to learn new technologies and maybe make contacts that can help you gain future employment.

Join a special-interest group (SIG) related to your technical expertise (fun, techie, will help at work)

The online social media can certainly expand your professional circles, but don't underestimate the professional value of participating in a SIG related to your technical expertise and/or passion. The discussions and presentations made at these meetings can greatly enhance your technical knowledge and expertise. You may also find it fun, based on the new like-minded people you will meet who are interested in this type of meeting.

Watch educational videos on YouTube and Vimeo rather than sitcom reruns (fun, techie, will help at work)

OK, fun is a stretch on this one, but how about also watching a couple of fun YouTube videos and we'll call it even. Regarding educational videos, the quantity of quality educational material on YouTube is remarkable. Use it to expand your technical and business knowledge.

In closing, I hope I have answered your question in a way that is of value to you. The trick here is to keep learning and keep participating. It's good for you, good for your career, good for the world, and maybe even a little bit of fun.

Until next time, work hard, work smart, and continue to grow.

ENHANCING YOUR NONTECHNICAL SKILL SET

As a techie, don't underestimate the value of soft skills. The ability to properly communicate with others, motivate fellow techies, and work with IT professionals and business users alike can be of great value professionally. Generally speaking, people working within IT self-selected to be in IT because of their technical ability and love for technology. That being the case, with rare exception, your technical ability alone will not differentiate you from the crowd or help you get promoted. The reason is that everyone in IT has technical ability and loves technology. If they didn't, they wouldn't be there. That said, it's your nontechnical soft skills combined with technical ability that will get you noticed and promoted.

The four columns contained in this section embody this concept of enhancing your hard skills with soft skills from differing perspectives.

The first column in this chapter, "Ten soft skills every business analyst needs," wasn't based on a specific reader question. I wrote this column based on seeing dozens of programmers over the years, including myself, try to make the move from programmer to business analyst as a way of moving ahead professionally into the management ranks. The issue was that they were very technical by nature and enhanced their raw technical abilities with years of technical training and professional experience. Their problem was that even if they were outgoing and people oriented, and some were not, they found that they lacked the necessary skills and training to effectively pivot to business-analyst-type roles. To right this wrong, these programmers began taking classes on software development methodology, active listening, influencing without authority, and other soft-skills-related classes. Then, with this non-technical training complete, they found that they were ready to make this move toward the next professional milestone.

When this column was originally published, it was immediately a hit. In fact, it has also been one of my most popular columns month after month since its original publication. I originally found this column's continued popularity to be very surprising. Upon deeper consideration, however, I realized that I shouldn't have been surprised, because I wrote this column based on my understanding of this programmer-to-business-analyst phenomenon.

I believe that a second reason for this column's popularity was the desire of business analysts to improve their skills, and I truly hope that this column has helped them to do so.

My column "Five important presentation tips for techies" was inspired by a question from a .NET programmer who was asked to do a presentation to senior management. He was excited to be asked, but it seems that at some point he realized that he didn't know how to write or give presentations in general, let alone to senior managers.

I have to say that it seems he had good instincts that a strong presentation would not only be a good professional experience, but it could also lead toward eventual promotion and/or assignment to other top projects.

The ability for a techie to make a quality presentation is not that important to all techies, only those who aspire to be business analysts, program managers, IT managers, or who wish to be seen as thought leaders in their technical expertise.

My next column highlighted in this chapter, "The hard skill/soft skill debate for techies," is truly an age-old debate of which I personally could have been the poster child. I started my professional career as a software developer, programming everything from COBOL to C to various other computer languages that have long since become obsolete and are only remembered in the minds of those who were forced to learn and use them. That said, I truly believed, even as a manager into my thirties, that soft-skill classes had no value as compared to the technical knowledge I gained in hard-skill-related classes. The problem was that I was wrong, as are so many other techies—particularly those techies who aspire to be managers.

I give enormous credit to the students taking my company's IT manager training classes. They know what I didn't learn until much later in my career—the importance of soft-skills training prior to and/or as you move into the management ranks.

Last but not least, the final column in this chapter, "Embrace your dormant skills and abilities," primarily discusses soft skills, but the concept can be applied to any new personal challenge. The idea is that to move ahead professionally, you will have to make strengths out of weaknesses, learn new skills, and develop new professional abilities in areas that currently intimidate you and/or make you nervous when you think about doing it. It may be public speaking, delegating tasks to others, giving presentations, learning to program in a new software language, or any other similar task that is currently outside your skill set, but is required to get you where you want to go. My recommendation to you is go for it. It can make you stronger. It may make you less afraid of trying new things. It may give you added self-confidence by moving beyond a longstanding roadblock, or help get you promoted. The true question here is, what would you try if you knew you would not fail?

Now, enough for my commentary; enjoy the columns.

TEN SOFT SKILLS EVERY BUSINESS ANALYST NEEDS

―――――――――

If you are in a typical business analyst role, you live in two worlds. You have one foot in the specified business area you are supporting and the other foot in IT. Even worse, often you have to keep the peace when IT and your business users don't get along.

There are a number of soft skills that would be well worth your while to master. These include the following:

1. Negotiation skills: These will be of value when facilitating negotiations between IT and business users, you and IT regarding development resources, and you and the business users trying to minimize project scope creep.

2. Active listening: This will be of great value when trying to collect business requirements, provide quality internal client service, and when gathering information for status reports.

3. Dealing with conflict: This will be of value when IT and users disagree and/or when deadlines are being missed and tensions are running high.

4. Quality client service techniques: As a representative of the IT community, providing quality client service to the business users you support is critical to your job performance and career advancement.

5. Decision making: There are many formalized decision-making techniques, such as a decision matrix, that can help you make quality, business-appropriate, and defendable decisions that can help you to best service your internal clients and maximize your job performance.

6. Problem solving: Like decision making, there are formalized problem-solving techniques, such as Five Whys and brainstorming, that can help you discover a problem's root cause and define potential solutions.

7. Strategic thinking: Very often a business analyst must think outside the box to find innovative business solutions that meet their internal clients' needs. An understanding of strategic thinking techniques can help facilitate this process.

8. Technical writing: A key role of business analysis is the creation of business requirement specifications and other forms of documentation. Your ability to develop coherent, informative, and usable documents is a requirement for professional success.

9. Presentation and public speaking: Don't underestimate the value of creating and delivering quality presentations on topics such as application designs, project status, and business requirements. Generally speaking, the people listening to your presentations are senior IT and business management people. Your ability to impress them with your presentation could have a significant effect on your career growth.

10. Team building: As a business analyst, you may be required to lead formalized and/or ad hoc teams. Your ability to structure, coordinate, and lead these teams can not only make you more successful in your current role, but position you for future IT senior positions.

Until next time, work hard, work smart, and continue to grow.

FIVE IMPORTANT PRESENTATION TIPS FOR TECHIES

The question I was asked:

Help! I'm a .NET developer and was just asked to make a formal thirty-minute presentation to senior management on the business intelligence system I just built. What do I do?

My answer:

First, congratulations on the new software you built. If you were asked to present it to senior management, then it must be very good. Well done!

To your question regarding your upcoming presentation, consider the following:

1. At a high level, begin your presentation with a short (five minutes maximum) PowerPoint-based overview of the system's overall data and functionality, followed by a live demonstration of the system, and ending with a short question/answer session.

2. Regarding your short (yes, I said "short" again because it's really important) opening PowerPoint, you could potentially include the types of slides listed below. When reviewing this list, note that the goal here is simply

to give your audience a context that enables them to understand (and appreciate) the live demonstration of the system.

    a. **Slide 1: An opening slide contains the system's name and your name.** This is important to orient your audience as to what you will be showing them. A typical senior manager's day is going from meeting to meeting. As a result, it would be good to remind him/her why he/she is there.

    b. **Slide 2: A very high-level overview of the data contained in the system.** As an example, this slide could say the system includes company financials, sales forecasts/pipeline, inventory levels, staffing levels, market share statistics, etc.

    c. **Slide 3: A very high-level overview of the system's primary functionality.** As an example, this slide could say the system has standardized reports, ad hoc reporting capabilities, drill-down capabilities, advanced analytics, etc.

    d. **Slide 4: Ask for high-level questions and move directly to the live system demonstration.**

5. For the live demonstration portion of your presentation (about twenty minutes) consider the following:

    a. **Plan out and practice your demonstration ahead of time.** Plan out and practice your presentation keystroke by keystroke and mouse click by mouse click. That way, when you practice (again, again, and again), you can develop a good flow and quality verbal commentary.

b. **Do not deviate from your planned demonstration.** During your presentation, follow your rehearsed plan. If you are asked a question outside your plan, answer it and then return to your plan. This will save you from accidentally hitting a software bug that aborts the application, showing an example that doesn't really work, displaying data you can't explain, and/or other ugly and unwanted outcomes.

c. **Use examples that your audience will relate to.** For example, if the VPs of Finance, Human Resources, and Sales are there, use one example from each area. You could show a finance report, Human Resources report, and sales forecasts.

d. **Illustrate system functionality as part of your relevant examples.** Following on the example above, you could show a standardized finance report, an ad hoc Human Resources report, and a drill down into the company's sales forecasts.

e. **Explain your navigation.** Each time you click the mouse or press the return key, tell your audience that you are doing so. This will help them understand and follow your presentation.

f. **Keep it high level.** Don't dig into minor technical points; you don't have the time. If you are asked a low-level question, answer it quickly, specifically, and move on.

g. **Remember you are presenting, not teaching.** Remember that the goal of your presentation is to impress and inform them, not teach them how to use it. You don't have time for detailed instruction; that comes later, after they are impressed and informed, and have more time.

h. **Talk functionality, not technology**. Unless you are asked a specific technical question, tell them what you built, not how you built it. If they are not techies, they won't care and most likely won't understand it even if you told them.

i. **Finish your demo on time.** Be very respectful of your audience's time. If you plan the demo for twenty minutes, finish it in twenty minutes. This will give you time to properly end your presentation.

6   **Close your presentation gracefully.** Once your live presentation is completed (about twenty-five minutes into your allotted half hour), ask if they have any quick questions, offer to follow up with them at another time if they want more information, and thank them for their time and interest.

7   **Leave time open after the formal presentation for questions.** Those who need to leave will do so. Those who want to leave will do so. However, those who want to stay and have the time may stay and ask you follow-up questions. Plan time on your calendar to stay a little longer so you won't feel pressured to cut your audience short.

Until next time, work hard, work smart, and continue to grow.

THE HARD SKILL/SOFT SKILL DEBATE FOR TECHIES

OK, I admit it. I was the biggest offender of the advice I am suggesting to you here.

As an individual contributor, I never took soft-skills classes. I loved training, but if I couldn't pick up an additional technical tip or two, I wasn't interested.

For many years, if I had the choice between Oracle Database Internals, Advanced Techniques in Function Overloading, or Active Listening, guess which two courses I took? Well, I'll give you a hint. It wasn't Active Listening or other soft-skills-related classes. I'm really glad I took the hard-skills classes, the technical information I learned helped me grow as a technical professional.

In retrospect, however, I believe I was less effective in a number of soft-skills-related areas than I would have been if I understood that even as a techie, these classes provided great value. That said, I should have also taken the soft-skill classes for the following reasons:

- All techies are smart and good technically, so it can be very hard to differentiate yourself from the pack. Quality soft skills can help you make that differentiation.
- Classes like Negotiation Skills can help you negotiate project scope, delivery dates, resources such as people and software

tools, and other things that can make projects more successful and, dare I say, more fun.
- Client-service-related classes can help provide the insights into how best to help the business users you support.
- If you want to move into a technical manager role, the sooner you develop/enhance these skills, the sooner you can get promoted and make money on it.

From a management perspective, as I moved into the management ranks, I didn't voluntarily take my first soft-skills-oriented class until I was an IT director. Truth be told, if I had attended these types of classes when I first became a technical lead, my road to IT management would have been a lot less bumpy for the following reasons:

- Being a technical manager is a very different profession from being an individual contributing techie, they have different challenges and require different skills.
- As a technical manager, communication is king. Understanding how to manage up, navigate company politics, and keep your business users satisfied all requires effective communication, strong listening skills, writing skills (even if just in e-mail), presentation skills, and other similar competencies.
- Your abilities to motivate, lead, and manage staff are all soft-skill-related activities and will play a key role in your future success in the management ranks.

Please understand my intent here regarding taking soft-skills-related classes. I'm not saying don't take hard-skill classes; take as many as you can. As a technical manager, they are still very good for you. They help you maintain your technical knowledge and keep you abreast of constantly moving technologies, even if you are no longer performing hands-on technical tasks. My goal here is to suggest that you also consider adding soft-skill training to your learning regimen.

There are a number of places you can get great soft-skills training even if your department doesn't have it in the budget or if you are currently not working:

- If employed, your company very possibly has internal instructor-led or online classes that are not cross charged to your department budget.
- If employed, your company very possibly provides tuition reimbursement for business-related classes, even soft skills, if appropriate to your job.
- If unemployed, various state agencies (varying by state) and nonprofit organizations offer free or almost free training classes.
- Regardless of your current employment status, there are very high-quality materials on YouTube, Wikipedia, and other information-oriented websites.

Until next time, work hard, work smart, and continue to grow

EMBRACE YOUR DORMANT SKILLS AND ABILITIES

As you grow professionally, you will find the need to learn new skills. Some of these skills, of course, will be technical in nature. Other skills, however, may be totally outside your technical areas of expertise.

For example:

- You're a programmer and are asked to write a user manual for a software product you created.
- You are a business analyst at a software company and are asked to make a sales presentation to a new potential customer about software you designed.
- You are a database administrator and are asked to speak at a Microsoft SQL server conference.
- You are an individual contributor and are asked to become a manager.

All of these scenarios force you to use skills that you have not yet polished or, at worst, use raw personal abilities you didn't know you had. When these situations arise, they can be a little scary, but if you embrace the moment, you may:

- grow as a person;
- grow as a professional;

- find you love doing something you never before thought you would enjoy;
- position yourself for a job promotion;
- find you have the ability to do things you once thought were undoable.

Early in my career, this happened to me. I was a new technical manager at a software company and was asked to work with the sales team to demonstrate software my group developed to potential new customers. I had no sales training and had never presented in front of clients. In short, I felt unqualified and very nervous. I found that with a little training, a little coaching, and a little practice, I did a pretty good job. In time, actually I found myself looking forward to making these presentations. Before being asked to participate in these sales calls, I would have never thought I could do this well, and I certainly never thought that I would have enjoyed it.

The moral of the story is that you, too, if given the opportunity to do something outside your comfort zone, may find that a previously uncomfortable endeavor may actually become a primary skill.

Another advantage of embracing new skills is that they may bring you in new and exciting professional directions you would not have previously expected. For example, you may find you like software testing better than software development. You may find technical management more interesting than being a hands-on techie. Alternatively, you may find, after giving a few presentations or managing a small team, that you truly love being an individual contributing techie and want to stay that way. All of these situations have value to you as a person and as a professional. It is, of course, great to find something new and exciting to move toward professionally. It's also, however, of great value to try something and decide it's not really right for you. This second case teaches you a little about yourself and removes a "what if I did that" from your professional journey.

Until next time, work hard, work smart, and continue to grow.

JOB SEARCH TIPS

———————

The inspiration for the columns highlighted in this chapter came from a number of sources. A couple of the columns are based on questions sent in by readers. One is based on a presentation I give on a regular basis to people in transition (between jobs). The others were based on a combination of job-hunting tricks I was told over the years and topics that were suggested to me by job hunters participating in my classes and seminars.

This section is very important to me because I have been in transition three times in my career. I was laid off twice and once was a casualty in a major senior management reorganization. During these times I was blessed with great advice from wonderful people who wanted to help me secure new employment.

I have also always done my best to help people find new jobs because of a situation I was involved in early in my career. I was the head of PC development at a software company. Truth be told, I loved that company and I, and hundreds of others like me, would still be working there today if the merger I'm about to talk about never happened. It was the mid-1980s and I was working in Boston. Our parent company bought our major competitor, based in Atlanta, and then merged us into them. I kept my job, but the entire graphics arts group (part of marketing) was laid off. Because of the graphical nature of their jobs, they actually had the biggest and best PCs in the company. The group was told about their layoff at nine o'clock one weekday morning and was told they had fifteen minutes to pack their personal belongings and leave the building. They were given very appropriate severance packages but had to leave the building quickly. Then, because I was head of PC development, I was immediately called and told to evaluate their PCs to see if my department could take advantage of any of their high-powered, abandoned PCs.

When I went to the old graphic arts group area, I could still almost feel their presence in the room. It was more like they were in a meeting than that they had been removed from the company. Because they had to leave so quickly, they didn't clean up the area or put away their work; they simply grabbed the pictures of their spouses and kids, other personal items, and headed to the door.

I had to sit at their desks, take notes of what software was installed, the size of the disk drives, the CPU speed, the amount of memory, and other similar statistics. Then, I had to go through their desk drawers looking for install disks and software manuals. Truth be told, I felt like I was violating their personal space because there were still half-full cups of coffee on the desks, drawers full of previously important work documents, and the first seat I sat in was still warm.

With this ordeal complete, I then returned to my office to find out the people in the offices on my left and right had been told about their removal, and I had not had a chance to say good-bye.

From that time forward, because of this experience, I have always tried to help people who were out of work and trying to find new employment.

The first column in this section is "How to find a job working remotely—it's easier than you think!" It was originally called "The IT world is also flat. Work at home from a thousand miles away." This column came about based on a discussion I had with a techie who said that he hadn't lived in the same city that he worked in for almost ten years. I asked him what it was like doing that much travel. He smiled and told me he didn't know. He went on to say that he had never met in person with most of the people he worked with, including his bosses and his staff. He said that the nature of his technical work could just as easily be done remotely as done in person. As a result, when he looked for new jobs, he looked worldwide, rather than just within driving distance, and he was almost always able to find work quickly and at a pay rate he thought was fair and appropriate. It also, for the most part, allowed him to work flexible hours as long as he was able to call in to specific scheduled meetings and got his work done on time.

The next column, "When to take old information off your resume," was based on a question I received from a reader. He seemed to be a very knowledgeable and accomplished techie and had about thirty years of professional hands-on experience. He said that his resume was about eight pages long because he thought that it was best to include all the projects he worked on and all the technologies he ever worked in as a way of illustrating his deep and strong understanding of technology and science-related applications. I answered his question via e-mail and then used my answer to him as the basis for this column.

If you are currently looking for a job or know someone who is, suggest that he/she read my next column, "Ten innovative places to find a great IT job." The essence of this column, and my advice to you, is do not just look for a new job in the same places as everyone else; be more innovative. There will be less competition and you may find the perfect job.

The column "Entrepreneurship can help you find a job" is based on a speech I give at no cost to nonprofit organizations that assist people in finding new jobs. At time of this writing, I have probably given this talk fifteen or twenty times. The talk is based on my personal experience after being laid off. I made a deal with myself that I would simultaneously look for a job and try to start a company and do whichever one happened first. Through this process I learned how entrepreneurship can actually help your job search.

I don't quite know what to say as an introduction of the column "Twenty-three resume-writing tips for techies." Its name is self-evident. My hope is that as you read through this column, you will find a few items that are of value to you.

The last column in this chapter is "Four ways to combine web-based and face-to-face-based job hunting for great results." The thrust of this column and the important takeaway for you is to not limit your job search to online media only. There is enormous value in networking face to face with people at various professional venues. In doing so you may hear about potential jobs that are not yet posted online or meet someone who is so impressed with you that he/she gets permission to hire you even though there are currently no officially open positions. This is referred to as an "opportunistic hire." So get out there and meet people—it may land you the job of your dreams.

Now, enough for my commentary; enjoy the columns.

HOW TO FIND A JOB WORKING REMOTELY—IT'S EASIER THAN YOU THINK!

Well, as the Bob Dylan song goes, "The Times They Are a-Changin'." In IT, more so than other professions, it's possible to find a job anywhere in the world and do that job from wherever in the world you happen to be.

The job search mentality for the last five thousand years or so has been to find a job near where you live, or where you want to live. The other rule of thumb during this same time has been if there are no jobs where you live, move where there are jobs.

As Thomas Friedman explained in his book *The World Is Flat*, we now live in a global rather than local economy. Couple this concept with the increased willingness of companies to allow employees to telecommute and you have it. They may be hard to find, but there are a large number of IT-related jobs nationwide or worldwide that could potentially be yours.

I'll give you two small examples from my personal experience to illustrate this point. My company built a virtual training building in Second Life. We thought we could do the automation inside the building, but needed a company specializing in Second Life to help us design and build our classroom. The company we found was about three hundred miles away, and their team included architects, software developers, interior designers, and others. They are literally located all around the world. I never met any of them in person. If fact, many of them had never met in each other in person.

As a second example, I have spoken to people who provide customer technical support for large companies from the comfort of their home. I don't think I should say the name of the company, but I'll simply say if you heard the name you would know it. I learned this because whenever I call technical support for anything, I always ask where they physically are. I asked this question one day and the answer I got was, "In my basement with my new puppy."

The trick for you is to analyze your skill set to define how the work you do can effectively be done remotely. Once defined, the world can be your workplace and your home can be your office.

Until next time, work hard, work smart, and continue to grow.

WHEN TO TAKE OLD INFORMATION OFF YOUR RESUME

The question I was asked:

I've been in IT for a long time and am currently updating my resume. I'm not sure what things I should/should not include from the early part of my career. Any advice?

My answer:

Generally speaking, unless it's relevant to a specific job you're applying for, details over fifteen years old or so are not of great value.

If you don't feel comfortable removing prior job experience from your resume, just include the job title, company name, and date employed. This approach still shows that you have significant experience, but thins out the size of your resume and emphasizes your more current work.

Also, regarding the hardware, software, application languages, and operating systems you have experience in, only include those that are relevant to today's world. For example, I was quite expert in the Digital DEC 10 operating system in 1980. This would have no value on my current resume.

Lastly, if your prior (very old) experience was as a programmer and your more recent experience (last fifteen years or so) has been as a manager or project leader, emphasize your leadership and/or project management positions and provide less detail on the now-less-relevant historical programming experience.

Thinning out your resume has another potential advantage. It provides you with the opportunity to add new, more current, and more relevant information to your resume without increasing its overall size. As an example, let's say your current resume is two pages in length and you want to keep it that way. If you can remove half a page of old and/or unneeded material, you will have the room to add a half page of newer, more job-relevant information without extending its overall length.

Personally, I found taking old information off my resume to be very uncomfortable and counterintuitive. After all, I was proud of my past accomplishments. Then, a close friend suggested, well, told me, that my resume was too long and that my most current jobs did not have enough detail. After making the changes, even I had to admit that my resume was vastly improved.

Until next time, work hard, work smart, and continue to grow.

TEN INNOVATIVE PLACES TO FIND A GREAT IT JOB

The question I was asked:

I'm tired of looking for a job online and being one of a thousand applicants. Where else can I look for an IT job?

The answer:

Your decision to look beyond the job websites for new employment may be your first step toward finding a new job. The job sites are great; in fact, I used to work for one. The trick is to use the online job sites as one of your potential job sources, not your only source. That said, consider adding to your investigation some or all of the potential job sources listed below.

1. Companies doing lots of nontechnical hiring

Companies that are hiring a large number of non-IT people will most likely need a proportional number of IT staff to support these new hires and the business activities they were hired to perform.

2. Companies that just received venture capital

If a company receives a large influx of cash from a venture capital firm, it generally means two things. First, very smart people at a venture capital firm think the company's business plan and/or management team are strong enough to potentially build a strong company.

Second, the company now has a large amount of money to spend, and some of it may be to hire IT people.

3. The company that laid you off

As the economy is beginning to improve, your company may need to hire additional staff, particularly if they were very aggressive laying people off. Who better to hire than a great former employee?

4. Consulting firms working for your old employers

Who is more qualified to work on a company's IT project than a former company employee who helped build the software the consulting firm has been engaged to support?

5. Software vendors of products you know

If you have experience supporting a software vendor's application—for example, SAP—see if the vendor and/or consulting firms that support that software are hiring.

6. Specific local companies you would love to work for

Find three to five local companies you would love to work for and try to network your way in through your business contacts, friends, and others.

7. Local companies with a recent dramatic rise in stock price

Check the stock price of all publicly held companies in your area and see if any of their stock prices are dramatically rising. If they are, the company must be doing something right and, as a result, may be hiring.

8. Cloud-based vendors that support your industry

Cloud computing is a megatrend within our industry. As a result, many IT shops are starting internal cloud-based initiatives and many cloud computing based vendors are beginning to gain traction.

9. Companies with press releases relating to technologies you know

Very often vendors issue press releases when they win a major new account. Follow the press releases of the vendor projects you know and call the companies that have agreed to purchase their products.

10. Find a couple of headhunters you like and trust

Don't underestimate the contacts, influence, and value of a well-connected and experienced technical recruiter. He/she can assist you with your resume and interview ability and open doors for you with potential employers.

Until next time, work hard, work smart, and continue to grow.

ENTREPRENEURSHIP CAN HELP YOU FIND A JOB

0Have you ever wanted your own company or a small business on the side? If you are out of work and looking for a job, this may be a golden opportunity to get started. Entrepreneurship can provide you with new insights, new business contacts, enhanced professional credentials, improved marketability in your job search, and maybe even your own company.

Let me begin by saying by saying that my assumption is that you are trying to start a company in the same general business area where you are looking for a job. For example, if you are a PC tech looking for a job doing PC helpdesk support, then your company would be in the area of PC support, not canoe making.

Believe it or not, the topic of combining job hunting with entrepreneurship is somewhat controversial. Some people will agree and love the idea. Some people will strongly disagree and say that time spent not looking for a job will hurt your job search. That's OK. My goal is to provide you with food for thought.

Searching for a new job is hard work, but it's not forty-hour-a-week work. In most cases, its –twenty to thirty hours of serious job searching and ten to twenty hours of worrying and/or looking at the phone. At least that's how it was for me. Certainly continue to push hard on your job search, but spend your worrying and waiting time creatively, energetically, and constructively by trying to start your own firm. You will soon find that the initial preparations needed to start a company can dramatically enhance your job search.

When reviewing the following table, you will see that the entrepreneurial activities listed on the left directly correlate to the job-hunting activities listed on the right. As a result, these entrepreneurial activities can help give your job search direction, help keep your skills fresh, and help you stay engaged in your profession until you find a new job or your company is launched.

Entrepreneurial Activities	Job Search Assistance
Performing competitive analysis	
Identify your competition	= List of companies you can target for employment
Research pricing	= General industry knowledge
Define how competitors reach their clients	= How you can reach potential employers
Define your competitive advantages	= The best way to sell yourself to employers
Defining a high-level marketing plan	
Define target client types (large, startup)	= List of companies you can target for employment
Define target client industries	= List of industries you can target for employment
Define organizations to reach target clients	= Places you can network to find employment
Define your PR/networking strategy	= Ways to promote yourself in your job search
Performing a gap analysis	
What knowledge do I need to acquire?	= Increased knowledge makes you more marketable
What certifications do I need to get?	= Increased credentials makes you more marketable
What networking organizations should I join?	= Places you can network to find employment

When reviewing the previous examples, note that you don't have to tell anyone you are thinking about starting your own company unless you decide to move forward.

Until next time, work hard, work smart, and continue to grow.

TWENTY-THREE RESUME-WRITING TIPS FOR TECHIES

―――――――――

When looking for a new permanent job or contracting assignment, having a great resume has always been important. Given our current extremely competitive times, a high-quality resume has moved from being important to being crucial.

The resume tips below have been divided into three main areas: Form and Function, Content, and General Thoughts. Truth be told, the reason for this categorization is because this is how I, as a hiring manager, review resumes.

- Do other people review resumes differently than I do? Yes.
- Is my way better or worse than how other people review resumes? No, it's just one way.
- Would every hiring manager and/or job search consultant agree 100 percent with what I am about to say? No, I think they would agree with me on most of my comments, but may disagree with a few of my points.
- Would they be right to disagree with me? Yes, their thoughts are equally as valid as mine. In fact, this is what makes resume writing so difficult. Different people have different opinions and like different things. As a result, you get conflicting suggestions on what is best. Your goal is to listen to

me and other experts and make an informed decision on which advice works best for you.

Regarding a resume's form and function, consider the following:

1. Make sure your resume is neat and well organized (shows organization and structure).

2. Be sure everything is indented properly. (I'm a techie, I can't help myself. I dislike source code that's not properly indented, and I guess I have extended that to resumes.)

3. Use bullet points, not lots of text. (I personally like bullet points because they're easier and faster to read.)

Regarding a resume's content, I suggest the following dos and don'ts:

The Dos

4. Use the right keywords and technology names.

5. Use effective, action-based titles.

6. Describe your technical achievements factually without boasting.

7. Describe the business value related to your technical accomplishments.

8. Explain the benefits of your specific skill set.

9. Back up your qualities and strengths with example accomplishments.

10. List your job responsibilities only if you are in senior management role.

11. Include nonprofessional accomplishments only if they are impressive and significant.

The Don'ts

12. Don't include obsolete technologies unless strategically placed.

13. Don't include irrelevant information.

14. Don't include technologies you don't really know; it can raise questions regarding the technologies you really do know.

15. Don't include "no kidding" information.

16. Don't feel required to list all your work experiences.

17. Don't leave unexplained time gaps in your work experience. Potential employers will think the worst, or at least ask for clarification if they like you.

Next, there are some general tips that may be of value to you:

18. After you have proofread your resume, give it to two other people to review.

19. Avoid negativity. It only hurts you.

20. Customize your resume to best meet each potential job opportunity.

21. Honesty is the best policy. False statements on your resume can destroy your professional reputation.

22. Don't use slang words or expressions. The people reading them may not understand your meaning.

23. Your personal and professional social media profiles should be consistent with your resume content.

In closing, even if you have great contacts and a great job, I suggest you keep your resume updated for two reasons. The first reason is if that once-in-a-lifetime job shows up at your doorstep, you will be ready to apply. A second and less obvious reason is that there is something about updating your resume that makes you sit back and think about your career at a macro level. This occasional introspection about your career goals and direction can help assure that you stay pointed in the right direction toward your ultimate objectives.

Until next time, work hard, work smart, and continue to grow.

FOUR WAYS TO COMBINE WEB-BASED AND FACE-TO-FACE-BASED JOB HUNTING FOR GREAT RESULTS

The question I was asked:

I have my resume on all the job board sites, I'm continually looking online for open positions, and am e-mailing them my resume. I also participate actively on a couple of job search blog sites. I have been looking for a job for over six months and have only had three responses and one interview. What am I doing wrong?

My answer:

The better question to ask may be "What am I not doing?" Certainly the online job boards are a great place to look for a job. In fact, I previously worked at one. That said, don't underestimate the incredible value of looking for a job the old-fashioned way, face-to-face.

By face-to-face job hunting, I mean all non-web-based activities, such as:

- participating in professional organizations;
- participating in job-hunting groups;
- cold calling companies where you would really like to work to see if any openings are available;

- calling people you know who are working at companies where you would really like to work to see if any openings are available; and
- other similar person-to-person related activities.

Let's first look at the advantages and disadvantages of looking for a job via the web and then the advantages of looking for a job face to face. As you will see, they both have value, but because they have different advantages, the best way for you to find a job is to do both.

Top two advantages of an online job search:

- It's very efficient in regard to finding companies with job openings.
- It's easy to apply via online forms and/or e-mail.

Top two disadvantages of an online job search:

- Statistically, there is a very low chance of your getting an interview.
- You don't know if there is actually a potential job to be filled.

Top two advantages of a face-to-face job search:

- Having made a personal connection to the Human Resources group or hiring manager, you have a much higher chance of getting the job.
- If you made a good impression but didn't get the job, you have at worst expanded your professional network and, at best, will be called at a later time when another job opens.

Top two disadvantages of a face-to-face job search

- It's more work and more time consuming.

- It's a numbers game—you end up talking to many people that can't help you find a job during the effort to find a few people that can help.

My suggestion to you is to combine online and face-to-face job search activities to maximize your effectiveness. It will give you the advantages of both. That said, consider the following:

1. Use web searches to find companies that are hiring and then use face-to-face networking to find contacts at these companies that can help you get the job.

2. Target companies where you would like to work, use LinkedIn to identify people that work at those companies, and personally contact these people via phone call and/or e-mail.

3. Participate in active discussion boards and blog sites in the technical area where you are looking for a job, then personally contact people who comment favorably on your posts.

4. Write a blog in your professional area. If you get noticed, great; if not, you are building your personal brand and can talk about your blog at networking meetings and during job interviews.

Until next time, work hard, work smart, and continue to grow.

IN THE WORKPLACE

Following along with the chapters in this book, first we discussed enhancing your technical skill set. Then, we moved on to discuss the enhancement of your nontechnical skill set, that is to say, your soft skills. The third chapter then discussed tips, tricks, and advice on finding a job. This chapter now deals with issues that arise in the workplace.

The columns included in this chapter discuss a wide range of issues, from starting a new job on the right foot to a fun one, what not to do as a technical manager. What I like most about this chapter is that it's very tactical and provides advice on ways to deal with real issues that we often encounter in the workplace.

The first column, "Ten great ways to start a new IT job on the right foot," was inspired by a question that we all ask ourselves when we start a new job: "what things can I do to get off to a great start?" As with all columns, I hope you find this one to be insightful and of value to you. My thought is that you can use this column in three ways.

- First and most obvious, when you start a new job.
- Second, as a manager, helping the people you hire to be successful in their new job.
- Third, as the basis for advice you give to friends starting new positions.

As you will see, the major takeaways from this column are:

- There are things you can do prior to your first day of work that can help you be successful.
- When your job first begins, quickly learn your department's and company's culture. This will help protect you from accidently stepping on unseen political landmines.
- Quickly learn about the systems and methodologies you will be working with. This will help you be more productive more quickly.

The column "Does telecommuting make you invisible?" was also based on a reader's question and was very heavily read when it was first released. Telecommuting and its counterpart, managing virtual teams, are in many ways two sides of the same coin and are very hot topics in the workplace in general. This is true for a number of reasons, including the following:

- It's less expensive for a company to let people work from home because it doesn't have to pay for office space.
- Offering current company employees the option to work from home can reduce employee attrition and in many cases increase productivity.
- In many professions, such as phone-based tech support and customer service, companies are actually able to attract more highly qualified workers if they have the option to work from home.
- Companies can hire people from a wider geographic area if commuting to the office on a daily basis is not a requirement.
- Because companies can hire people from a wider geographic area, there is the potential to pay lower average wages by hiring people in lower-wage parts of the country and/or world.

In addition to all of the advantages listed above, most large companies now have offices throughout the world that need to work together on projects for the common company good. Therefore, even if you go into the office every day, your boss and those you work with may, very possibly, physically be in another city. I have a friend who had this situation. He worked in Boston within the IT group of a very large financial services firm. Even though he went into the office every day, he never physically saw his boss, his peers, his staff, or his business users because they all worked in different locations. As I recall, his boss was in one city and his staff, peers, and business users were sprinkled around dozens of locations around the world. After a while, he stopped commuting into the office and just worked from home, as did his boss and many of the others previously listed.

The column "Motivation: fourteen simple ways to motivate development teams" discusses one of the many issues you will face if you move into an IT supervisory or management role. Look at the advice in this column from two perspectives: first, as intended by the column, are ways to motivate your staff; second is to think about what motivates you. This second point is extremely important, because whether we are managers or individual contributors, we're still employees. Therefore, knowing what motivates you personally can dramatically improve your professional performance and simultaneously enhance your personal job satisfaction. That said, if there are things listed in this column that you believe would help motivate you, try to seek out managers, companies, and/or jobs that can provide you with these and other personal motivating factors.

The next column in this chapter is "Don't like your job? Define one you like," which suggests a rather interesting concept. As the title alludes, if you don't like your current job, but like your boss and the company where you work, try to define a new role for yourself which provides great value to your company and you professionally.

The column "What's on your laptop can be career limiting" wasn't based on a specific reader question. Its inspiration came from an article I read in my local newspaper about an issue at a company because an employee lost his laptop. I don't remember the specific industry, but the person was a software developer beginning the testing of a software module he had written. The problem was he was testing his software using real production data which contained clients' names, addresses, credit card numbers, and other extremely sensitive information. To make matters worse, neither the data nor the hard drive was encrypted.

I felt sorry for this employee because his goal was simply to bring work home so he could finish his project on time. The problem was, by doing so he damaged his company and may have lost his job. Based on this story, I decided to write this column with the hopes that it would help protect my readers from a similar fate.

The column "It's OK to say no" was actually based on a question from an IT manager, rather than an individual contributor. As you will read, he was being pushed due to unrealistic expectations by his business users. Anecdotally, this seems to be a problem in many IT shops. In essence, we become victims of our own success. We want to continually provide technical services faster, better, and cheaper to the business areas we support. The problem this creates is that those we serve, who in many cases don't really understand what we do, try to push us beyond what is actually possible. This puts us, as IT professionals, in a very bad position. On the one hand, we want to say yes because we truly want to provide the best possible value to our business groups. On the other hand, if you don't eventually say no, then bad things can happen, such as:

- missing deadlines;
- quality problems due to reduced development and testing time;
- becoming burned out because of an overwhelming workload;
- eventual loss in user confidence because of the above items.

This is why we must learn to sometimes say no, even if our natural inclination is to always say yes. At the end of the day, saying no may actually be in your user's best interest as well as your own. This column provides you some tips and tricks on how to say no respectfully in the workplace.

I love the concept discussed in the column "Overworked? Maximize your productivity by knowing your zone" because, at its core, it's not about dealing with the personal stress of being overworked. It discusses a great time management technique that I personally use on an ongoing basis. To be honest, it's this technique that has helped me achieve the level of personal productivity needed to simultaneously start a company, write weekly columns for both ITworld and Gatehouse Media, write this book, and still have a personal life.

Doesn't the next column, "Six ways to help manage your boss," sound great! Oh, and you still have to do what your boss says. On a serious note, at a high level, the column provides two pieces of advice: to do your best and to manage up effectively. If you can do these two things, well, then you are on your way to not only managing your boss, but one day being the boss.

The last column in this section, "The top ten ways to be a bad technical manager," does in fact have some valuable advice for technical managers, but it is presented in a really fun way. I got the idea for the format by watching the David Letterman show one night. I forget what the topic was, but it was well done and very funny. After the monologue, I turned off the TV and went to bed. About two o'clock that morning I woke up with the idea for this column, got a pencil and paper, wrote down my idea, and went back to sleep. When I woke up in the morning, I had totally forgotten about it until I saw what I had written, sitting on the kitchen table. It was only the title and two or three items, but it was enough to get me started.

Now, enough for my commentary; enjoy the columns.

TEN GREAT WAYS TO START A NEW IT JOB ON THE RIGHT FOOT

The question I was asked:

I just got a new job in a great IT organization. What things can I do to get off to a great start? Thanks, and I hope you publish my question. :)

Thanks,

Justin T.

My answer:

Hi, Justin, thanks for writing in. First and most important, congratulations on your new job. There are a number of things you can do to help assure a quality start to your new job. As you will see, some can be done before your first day of work, others can be done as early as your first day of employment, and they are all related to learning about your new work environment.

Things you can do prior to your first day of work.

1. **Learn as much as you can about the company,** including its products, locations, history, revenue, and number of employees. This can be done by a combination of studying the company's website, doing web and Twitter searches on the company's name and its product names, and, if the

company is publicly held, analyzing its stock price over the last year and any available investment research notes.

2. **Learn about the industry** if your new employer is in an industry you are not familiar with (for example, health care, financial services, construction, etc.). This will help you gain a better understanding of the environment in which your company operates.

3. **Use LinkedIn and other means to find someone who previously worked for the company.** By talking with an ex-employee, you can generally get an unbiased and honest opinion of the company, including internal politics, things to watch out for, and how to best succeed.

4. **Learn about the IT group's vendors, methodologies, and technologies** based on any information you gained during your interview process. Having a general understanding of these topics will save you a little study time once your job begins.

5. **Learn about the company's major competitors,** particularly if the company has a specific competitor that it considers an archrival. Knowing a little about the company's competitors may help you create innovative IT solutions that truly can help beat the competition.

Once you have started to work at the company, you will have access to additional information that can help you learn about your new job and department.

6. **Watch and learn the dynamics, politics, land mines, and general behavior of people within your IT department, and business users**. This will not only help you fit into the work environment more easily, but it will also help protect you from accidently making enemies.

7. **Find a copy of the company's organization chart** with the goal of understanding the formal structure of your department, IT as a whole, the business areas you support, and the company in total. This way, as you are introduced to your fellow employees, you will have a general understanding of their organization level and responsibilities. If the organization chart includes employee pictures, all the better. If you're not good at remembering faces, reviewing these pictures can be a great way of remembering who's who.

8. **Gain an understanding of your IT group's software development methodologies and key technical processes.** This will allow you do things right the first time and minimize your need for rework.

9. **Learn about your IT group's key systems and data flows.** This will give you a better understanding of how information is processed within the company. This understanding will help provide you with an overall framework of how the internal systems are architected and how your specific project fits into IT as a whole.

10. **Listen and learn before you speak.** As the new person on the block, I know I always wanted to immediately come up with new ideas and great suggestions. In truth, more often than not, I was off the mark because of my lack of background and knowledge of the company. I was the new guy. Definitely speak up, but not before you're ready. As the saying goes, God gave us two ears and one mouth, so we should listen twice as much as we speak.

Until next time, work hard, work smart, and continue to grow.

DOES TELECOMMUTING MAKE YOU INVISIBLE?

The question I was asked:

I work within a large IT organization, and the people in my department have been given the opportunity to work from home. If I do, does it reduce my opportunities for promotion and/or increase my chances of getting laid off?

My answer:

First, thanks for asking. It's great to get questions from my ITworld readers. In short, the answer to your question regarding the effect of telecommuting on promotions and layoffs is that it depends on the following:

- your company's culture and norms regarding telecommuting;
- the percentage of people at your company that work remotely;
- how visible you can be on a day-to-day basis to your boss and others;
- how effectively you can perform your job remotely.

Now let's discuss these items one at a time.

Your company's culture

Companies, like people, have specific values, strengths, weaknesses, prejudices, and, dare I say, personalities. That said, consider the following questions when deciding if you want to telecommute:

- Is the company technically equipped with conference room speakers, remote computer access, and tools needed to facilitate efficient work from outside the office?
- Does your company conceptually support telecommuting or does it simply tolerate it?
- Can you remotely participate in important department discussions?
- Is there an out-of-sight-out-of-mind mentality for those working out of the office?
- Is your boss supportive of telecommuting, or is he/she begrudgingly providing the option because it's company policy?
- Are virtual teams at your company managed well or managed poorly?

Percent of people working remotely

The reason I ask this question is that if a high percentage of people work from home and/or business groups are generally spread over multiple physical locations, then needed work-related processes are (or should be) in place to accommodate remote workers. If, however, you will be the only team member working remotely, you will most likely often be forgotten, not with any animosity, just due to people forgetting to call you. As previously said, you will be out of sight, out of mind.

How visible can you be from home?

The reason for this question is that some jobs, by their nature, are more connected to the people you work with than others. For example, if you are a software tester and are continually communicating with programmers, users, and other testers by e-mail, via formal bug reports, and by phone to discuss issues, you can be very internally visible. If, however, you write documentation or provide phone-based customer support, by the nature of your job, you will be less interactive with your boss and teammates. With this second scenario, it will be much harder for you to have high office visibility from home.

How effective can you be remotely?

Certain job types are better than others regarding working remotely. For example, generally speaking, it is easier for a programmer to work from home than for a business analyst if the business analyst needs to interview users as part of the writing a functional specification for a new software application.

There is one additional potential option for you. Instead of working from home all the time, consider splitting your time between telecommuting and working at the office. That is to say, work from home two or three days a week and the remainder of the time at the office. This could potentially give you the best of both worlds, some time working at home and some visibility at the office.

In closing, telecommuting can work out wonderfully for both you and your company if, and only if, the company and your job are structured in a way that facilitates its success.

Until next time, work hard, work smart, and continue to grow.

MOTIVATION: FOURTEEN SIMPLE WAYS TO MOTIVATE DEVELOPMENT TEAMS

The question I was asked:

I was just promoted from senior software developer to software development manager. What things can I do to motivate my team?

My answer:

First, congratulations on your promotion. I started my career as a programmer also and found the move to manager to be exciting, thought provoking, and sometimes a little bit scary.

As a bad takeoff on my favorite soft drink jingle, "I'm a techie, you're a techie, your staff are techies, too," so think about the things that motivate and excite you professionally. Many of these same things may also motivate and excite your staff. Over the years I have found that if I simply treat my staff like I would like to be treated, I'm doing most things right.

Specifically to your question regarding how to motivate your new team, at a high level, techies are generally motivated by two things: first, by the items that motivate all employees, such as a supportive manager, and second, by factors specifically related to their profession, such as the availability of state-of-the-art tools.

Now let's talk about these motivation types one at a time.

Regarding the items that motivate all employees, remember that techies are people, too. As a result, the following general items are motivating by their nature.

- Recognition of their ability
- Promotional opportunities
- A fair and pleasant workplace
- Work/life balance
- Recognition of work
- A supportive, fair, and competent manager

All employees also like to feel that they are being fairly compensated for time and expertise. As a result, the following items generally will not make them motivated, but will help keep them motivated.

- Competitive compensation
- Quality benefits like health insurance
- Tuition reimbursement
- Available funds to take training classes

From a techie-specific perspective, consider the following:

- Opportunity to expand skill set
- Opportunity to create
- Mental stimulation and challenge
- Opportunity to get your work done

Regarding the **opportunity to expand skill set**, it's my opinion that technology has a two year half-life. This means that the technologies you know today are only half as valuable to you professionally two years from now. Therefore, as techies, we must continually update our skill set.

Regarding the **opportunity to create**, to the extent possible, give your team the time and the tools to get their work done.

Regarding providing **mental stimulation and challenge,** to the extent possible, try to give your team interesting things to work on that will help expand their knowledge and abilities.

Lastly, regarding the **opportunity to get their work done**, try to protect your team from continuous interruptions. This will not only help their productivity, but it will enhance their sense of accomplishment.

Until next time, work hard, work smart, and continue to grow.

DON'T LIKE YOUR JOB? DEFINE ONE YOU LIKE.

The question I was asked:

I love the company where I work. The people are great, the benefits and salary are more than fair, and the company is doing well. My problem is that I'm tired of my current business analysis role and there don't seem to be any jobs opening internally that are appropriate for me. What do I do?

My answer:

They say that timing is everything. As a case in point, I began writing this answer while sitting in a coffee shop waiting to meet a fellow professional speaker. When he arrived, he asked me what I was working on. I showed him the above question I had received from a reader and, just by chance, he recently spoke on this topic. He said the following:

When you look only at your skills you become a commodity and/or a tool. When you focus on results, you become the expert that is called upon to solve existing problems. So look for other problems at your company where you can bring quality results. Your ability to solve these types of problems may be the basis for your next job at the company.

My friend's name is Stephen Balzac. He can be found at www.7stepsahead.com.

As additional food for thought, I would like to ask you a few questions.

- What do you like to do?
- What are the attributes of your ideal job?
- What are you currently qualified to do?
- With reasonable additional training, what would you be qualified to do?
- What potential job roles exist at your company that interest you and match your current or future skill set?

The combined answer to these questions can help provide you with the insights needed to map out your short-term and long-term job possibilities. It can also help you find and fill holes in your resume that are currently holding you back. It may also help provide you with the clarity needed to move you toward your ultimate professional aspirations.

With this knowledge in mind, try to combine it with Steve's thoughts on looking within your company for places where your skills can create positive, measurable results.

When looking for a new position, begin by looking within your current department. You may find that with a little thought and creativity, the opportunity you are looking for may exist within your current department. You may be able to grow your existing role in a way that helps your company and provides you with the professional growth you are seeking.

Trying to define your own job is not as farfetched as you may believe. I know people who have done it successfully. The trick to make it happen is to do the following:

- Do a great job in your current role so your manager and others will feel positive about you personally and the results you produce.
- Try to be a problem solver by nature. This will help make you the go-to person for your manager and others when problems arise.
- Be watchful for opportunities to improve internal department/company processes and work to improve them, when within your authority to do so.
- Be alert for opportunities to expand your existing role into areas that are good for the company, can help you grow professionally, are within your skill set, and are of interest to you.

Who knows, with vigilance, hard work, and a little bit of luck, your next job may be one of your design and making.

Until next time, work hard, work smart, and continue to grow.

WHAT'S ON YOUR LAPTOP CAN BE CAREER LIMITING

―――――――――

I know the readership of this column is a technical crowd. Don't worry, I'm not going to talk about computer viruses and other related technical issues.

If you're a software developer, tester, business analyst, or project manager, if you lose your laptop, leave it on the train, or it is stolen out of your car, the work files you have on your laptop can potentially get you fired.

For software developers, your risks include the release of

- test data containing real customer information, including credit card numbers, Social Security numbers, etc.;
- hardwired company passwords to FTP sites, cloud-computer-based applications, and firewall pass-throughs;
- source code to company proprietary algorithms, such as security schemes, mathematical formulas, stock/bond purchase algorithms, etc.;
- ompany internal data, such as customer lists, marketing plans, employee salary information, etc.;
- company proprietary source code that gives your company a competitive edge or is used in a software product if you work for a software company.

For testers, your risks include the release of

- all those things listed above for software developers if you are working closely with the software development teams;
- test plans that highlight potential weaknesses in client-/customer-facing software applications;
- functional and technical specification documents that contain information on company proprietary software applications, business processes, and implementation schedules;
- lists of problems with current project software that could be exploited for fraudulent purposes;
- lists of testing passwords that are live in production applications.

For business analysts, your risks include the release of

- all of those items listed above if you are working closely with the software developers and/or testers;
- documentation on key business processes, business initiatives, quotes and analysis of existing company problems, and issues from company executives and application users;
- business cases that include information on company initiates and new product releases.

For project managers, your issues include the release of

- names and contact info of key business and technical users;
- names of key developers, testers, business analysts, and users;
- project time frames and business initiatives.

The goal of the above lists is simply to illustrate the potential problems that could be caused for your company if your laptop is lost and ends up in the wrong hands. As you saw when reading these lists, good work is being done, all intent is ethical, and this type of information is probably on your laptop because you plan to work at home. The lesson is, don't get in trouble for working hard and trying to do the right thing.

- Be cognizant of what information is contained on your laptop.
- Use disk-level encryption installed in cooperation with your company's PC helpdesk.
- For those of you who are managers, assure that your team is also cognizant of these issues and potential safeguards.

In retrospect, earlier in my career, as a programmer, business analyst, and project manager, I believe there were times when I had information on my PC that could have caused problems for my company, and me, if my laptop had been lost or stolen. I don't think the rules and maybe even the risks were as well defined and/or as severe as they are now. Nevertheless, it would not have been pleasant. Don't let this happen to you. In today's world, it could cost you a promotion, a raise, a bonus, your job, and/or, in extreme cases, your professional reputation.

Until next time, work hard, work smart, and continue to grow.

IT'S OK TO SAY NO

The question I was asked:

I'm a software development manager who is continually being pushed by my business users to do more and do it faster, better, and cheaper. I can't keep up with their demands and I think it's putting my job in peril. Could I please have your advice on how to deal with this issue?

My answer:

This is a great question. My bet is that because of the nature of IT's role and the reduction of resources because of general economic conditions, this issue is on the minds of many IT professionals, tech leads, and managers around the country and around the world.

I think this issue can be addressed in a number of ways, including the following:

- Provide transparency to your business users regarding what your group's current projects and workload are.
- Once transparency has been achieved, work with your users to prioritize your team's work in a way that makes sense for both them and you.
- Find creative ways to say no to your business users in a way that they understand and accept.

The remainder of this blog post will discuss this third point.

Sometimes it's not what you say, it's how you say it. Learning to say no in an acceptable and positive way is one of these cases. Also, as an aside, learning to say no effectively is more than a tool for the workplace; it is also a life skill that can potentially help you in all aspects of your life.

This trick to saying no effectively is to do so in a nonargumentative manner that explains the reason why and suggests an alternative option. For example:

- Sorry, I can't commit to that right now because you have me working on other things. Would you rather that I did this first and delay my other deliverables?
- Yes, we can do that, but may I suggest that we do it this way instead?
- I don't think I'm the best person to work on that. May I suggest talking with Mary, as she is more knowledgeable than I on that topic?
- How is this task prioritized regarding the other tasks I am working on?
- Yes, this feature would be good for the application we are building, so let's put it in the next version of the software. This version is almost done, and I know you would like it completed as soon as possible.
- I don't think that will work because of…. May I suggest we do…instead?

The goal of the above statements is to frame them in a way that is of value to your business user and provides you with the time, task, and resources that allow you to be successful. This can best be explained by a saying I read on a Salada tea label many years ago: "The art of politics is letting other people have things your way."

As IT professionals, it is extremely important that we provide the highest quality service possible to the internal business groups we serve. High quality service is good for the company, your internal business users, your external clients, and you personally. That said, turning a "No, that can't be done" into a "Yes, but…" can be a win-win for everyone. That is to say, your business users get what they need and you have control on how the service is provided.

As a final note, like sports and all good management techniques, you can't win them all, but with the right coaching and a little practice, you can increase your winning percentage.

Until next time, work hard, work smart, and continue to grow.

OVERWORKED? MAXIMIZE YOUR PRODUCTIVITY BY KNOWING YOUR ZONE

The question I was asked:

Since my company's layoff last year, I've had more work than I can handle. I'm working really hard, but can't seem to keep up with it. Any thought on ways I can increase my productivity?

My answer:

Thanks for your question. My belief is that there are millions of other people asking the same question. I think the best way for me to answer you is to tell you what I do. I'm a big believer in working in your highest zone. The rest of this column will explain this statement.

Let me begin by explaining my concept of being in the zone. In the zone is being:

1. mentally clear on the task to be performed;
2. highly focused on a specific task;
3. physically able to perform the task;
4. motivated to perform the task.

By **mentally clear**, I mean having an exact understanding of what you want to do. It could be something simple, like deleting spam e-mail, or something intense, like designing the new structure for your company's communication backbone.

By **highly focused,** I mean single-minded, namely, being able to free yourself from mental distractions, like thinking about other projects, all the e-mails you must answer, or a presentation you are making later in the day.

By **physically able**, I mean that at this moment you are able to perform the task. For example, I know that if I'm very tired, I have great difficulty doing mentally challenging work like writing my columns, answering important e-mails in a concise manor, or making important decisions.

By **motivated**, I mean that this is a task that you want to (or have to) work on right now.

For me personally, and I know anecdotally from speaking with others, when people are truly in the zone on a task, regardless of the task's simplicity or complexity, you are more productive, more innovative, and do a better job. This powerful combination of productivity, innovation, and quality is why you, and I, should strive to be in the zone on any task we are performing.

Now, with these definitions in mind, **your highest zone** is the task at that time that best fits the above descriptions. Using a previous example, if I'm mentally exhausted and have two hundred e-mails to review, my highest-zone work at that time may be simply deleting spam and other irrelevant e-mails from my inbox. If I am mentally alert, the deadline for my next ITworld column is quickly approaching, and I have a great topic idea in mind, I'll write my column, even if my e-mail inbox is a mess.

Given these two examples of cleaning out my e-mail or writing my column, from a personal productivity perspective, it would be a mistake for me to spend my time deleting e-mails if I have the ability, motivation, and focus to write my column. I can delete my old e-mails later, when I am less mentally sharp.

The final lesson for you here is mentally dividing the items on your to-do list by zone levels. These levels could be:

1. when I'm at my best;
2. business tasks I can do on autopilot;
3. busy tasks that must be done but don't require mental challenge;
4. things you can do as long as you are not asleep.

Then, pick the task to be performed based on your physical, mental, and motivational status at that time.

Until next time, work hard, work smart, and continue to grow.

SIX WAYS TO HELP MANAGE YOUR BOSS

The first thing you must do to properly manage your boss is to be the best employee you can be.

You must:

- do quality work;
- embrace company values;
- meet your deadlines;
- play well in the company sandbox; and
- generally be a true asset to your department.

With these things now in place, you have the opportunity to manage your boss. That said, when reading the following potential ways to manage your boss, note that you should choose your tactics wisely based on your relationship with him/her, your role within your department, and the culture of your organization.

1. When you bring issues to your manager, also provide potential solutions and your suggested recommendation. With a well-thought-out recommendation in hand, you will very likely be able to correct the issue in the manner you wish.

2. Try to view the world from your manager's perspective. This will not only help you better understand your manager's

needs and wants, it will also help your professional growth should you hope, in time, to attain your manager's position.

3. Be transparent with your manager. That is to say, be equally willing to tell him/her about the good news as well as the bad news. This approach of sharing both good and bad news has many advantages, including the following:

   d. It develops trust from your manager toward you.

   e. When you give your boss good news, he/she will believe you because he/she knows that you are also willing to admit bad news.

   f. It allows you to get advice from your boss on issues requiring action. This advice will not only help you correct your problem, but it will also help you grow professionally by allowing you to gain knowledge as to how your boss would handle the issue.

   g. It allows you to take credit for correcting a difficult problem because you are willing to tell your boss, in the first place, that a problem was in need of attention. In essence, you can't get credit for correcting a problem if your boss never knew that the problem existed.

4 Be a department thought leader regarding department processes and technologies. This will help make you more valuable to your department and, in turn, to your manager. This added value will (or should) cause your manager to take your opinions and recommendations seriously, thus making your suggestions more likely to be accepted.

5 Begin to think both tactically and strategically. This combination of a short-term and long-term perspective will help you create and present better ideas and suggestions to your

manager, thus making the implementation of your solutions more likely.

6 Consider issues from both a technical and nontechnical perspective. Like thinking tactically and strategically, this dual perspective will help you define and present better potential solutions and recommendations.

In closing, the way to best manage your boss begins with being the best employee you can be, grows by gaining your manager's trust, and concludes by creating innovative and well-thought-out solutions to department problems that you would like to solve based on your recommendations.

Until next time, work hard, work smart, and continue to grow.

THE TOP TEN WAYS TO BE A BAD TECHNICAL MANAGER

───────────────

As technical professionals, almost all of us have worked with managers that just can't seem to get it right. It's almost like they have been specially trained to be bad managers. That said, maybe they just read the list below. Enjoy. :)

10. Tell your Java programmers how much you like .NET and vice versa.

9. Gossip about your staff on your Facebook page and in the restroom without checking to see that no one is in the stalls.

8. Put next year's salary plan on your whiteboard and forget to erase it before having a staff meeting in your office.

7. Tell your team that you love the TV show *Big Bang Theory* but can't relate to any of the characters.

6. Have really boring weekly staff meetings and make them three hours long.

5. Take credit for great technical work done by your staff members, even if you have no clue how the work was done.

4. Make your helpdesk staff wear strict business attire—suits and ties for the men and skirt suits for the ladies.

3. Schedule a lunch meeting and forget to order the food.

2. Specialize in reverse compliments, like "Great job! It was nice to see you didn't screw up this project also."

1. Name your network servers after *Star Trek*, *Star Wars*, and *Matrix* characters and spell all the names wrong.

Until next time, work hard, work smart, and continue to grow.

MAXIMIZING YOUR PAY

As the title suggests, the three columns in this chapter deal with compensation-related issues, but from very different angles. The first column is of concern to any techie who doesn't want to move into the management ranks. The second column discusses various advantages and disadvantages of moving from a contractor status to an employee status. The third column essentially asks the question, "Can changing your job title can bring you additional prestige and higher pay?"

The title "Can techies increase their salaries without becoming managers?" asks an age-old question for technologists of all types. This column discusses the compensation pluses and minuses of staying a techie and, if you decide to stay technical, the things you can do to maximize your pay.

The column "Contract programmer considers permanent employment" was one of my first columns and is in the shorter format. It was based on a question from a reader. He said that he had been working as a contractor for a number of years and his current client asked him to join the company as an employee. My answer was designed to outline many of the pros and cons of each to help the reader make an informed decision on this potentially life-changing event.

The last column in this chapter, "Can the job title 'data scientist' raise your pay?" on its face discusses the validity of the data scientist job title for those doing data visualization, data mining, and data-driven statistical analysis. It then goes on to question if this change in job title is just a title or a conduit to a larger paycheck.

At a deeper level, this last topic suggests a far more reaching question. Are there specific skilled jobs within the IT profession that should be classified by corporations more as a science than simply as an IT-related skill set? The answer to this question has far-reaching implications to the individuals with the skill sets being discussed and those hoping to work in these areas in the future, including the following:

- Will the compensation for these skill sets increase?
- Will PhD degrees be required to be recognized as an expert within these roles?
- Will these skill sets remain within IT or be moved to another part of the company?
- If the data scientist job title catches on, what effect will it have on other analytical roles within IT?
- Will new certifications arise as a way of solidifying the credentials of these new roles?

Bringing this last topic back to you and out of the stratosphere, I would like to ask you a few questions specifically regarding your job and its associated job title.

- Does your job title accurately reflect the type of work you actually do?
- Is your current job title so generic that it provides you with no value on your resume or when trying to establish your professional brand?

- Is there a more impressive, but equally accurate job title you could use that could be of value to you at your company, on your resume, and/or toward establishing your professional brand?

Now, enough for my commentary; enjoy the columns.

CAN TECHIES INCREASE THEIR SALARIES WITHOUT BECOMING MANAGERS?

───────────

AKA, Management track vs. staying technical

The question I was asked:

I'm currently a Java technical lead at a large financial services company. My problem is that I love being a hands-on software developer but believe I have to go into management to increase my pay. Is this true and what do you suggest?

My answer:

To begin with, I wanted to answer you in my column, rather than via a personal e-mail, because your question hit home for me. I ultimately decided to move into a management role because I found that I liked being a manager. The difficult part for me was the fear of losing my technical skill. What I didn't realize until I became a manager is that, like being a techie, being a manager requires a specific skill set that grows and matures over time. That said, as a way of trying to maintain my technical edge, I taught technical classes at a local university for almost fifteen years.

It has long been debated within the technical community whether the choice to stay technical can provide the same levels of compensation and organizational ranking as those who move into management roles.

To answer your question directly, it has been my experience that there are very few individual contributors in very few companies, technical or nontechnical, who achieve salary and organizational parity with their management-oriented counterparts.

That said, if you are an exceptional techie and appreciated within your company, it is very possible to have equal or greater compensation than a first-line supervisor or manager. This parity, however, becomes much less likely when comparing an individual contributor to a middle-level or upper-level manager.

If you choose to stay an individual contributor, the key to maximizing your compensation is to be the very best techie you can be.

- Be a thought leader in your specific technical area.
- Be the primary contact for the company's most important software application.
- Become the company's lead expert in the technical direction in which the company is moving, for example, the development of companywide private cloud.
- Become known as an industry leader in an industry-specific technology, and become a spokesperson for your company at important industry conferences.

Next, I would like to make a distinction between working in internal IT and working in technical product engineering (PE), a software group that develops software for sale or as part of an online product offering.

There is the potential to achieve VP-level status as technical individual contributor within both IT and PE. However, based on my personal anecdotal knowledge and not based on any specific statistical rigger, the PE-type groups tend to have more VP-level techies than IT groups. I think this is true because technical products for sale often have/need senior technologists in roles that are designed to help the company's sales and marketing organizations sell the product. These roles include:

- chief product architect (from a marketing perspective);
- technical product spokesperson;
- product marketing—feature specialist;
- presales specialist;
- product implementation specialist; and
- other similar roles that are a blend of technology, sales, marketing, and product implementation.

In closing, at the end of day, we spend almost one third of our life working. It should be something that you love to do and look forward to when you wake up in the morning. If you love being a techie and hate the idea of becoming a manager, stay a techie and become the best techie you can be. If you think becoming a manager is right for you, then work to become a great manager. All technical organizations, regardless of the industry they service, need both great techies and great technical managers.

Until next time, work hard, work smart, and continue to grow.

CONTRACT PROGRAMMER CONSIDERS PERMANENT EMPLOYMENT

―――――――――

The question I was asked:

For the past ten years I have successfully worked as a contract programmer. The company I'm currently working with has asked me to come on board as a permanent employee. If I take the job, what differences can I expect as an employee?

My answer:

There's good news and bad news when moving from a contactor role to a permanent employee.

Let's start with the good news of being a company employee. There is the potential for promotion. You will become part of a long-term team. You'll most likely be provided benefits, such as health, life, and disability insurance. You'll be given the opportunity to participate in retirement programs like 401(k)s. Your employer will be paying half of your Social Security tax. Lastly, you may be given the opportunity to learn new technologies via internal company initiatives and/or formal training classes.

Now let's discuss the bad news. You'll have little or no flexibility regarding the projects you work on and your work schedule. Also, you will meet fewer people, because you will be working with the same team on multiple projects, rather than changing teams, companies, and/or industries on a project-by-project basis.

You will also see some dramatic changes in your compensation. The things you consider positive or negative with this change are primarily based on your current financial position, your long-term goals, and your ability to get health insurance for you and your family from other sources.

To begin, as an employee, the cash amount in your paycheck will go down because your compensation is not just cash based, but also includes insurance benefits, retirement benefits, paid vacation, paid holidays, tuition reimbursement, and other similar items. When you add up the value of all these benefits, your total compensation may be higher, but your cash-in-pocket may be significantly less.

Also consider that while it's great that companies provide health insurance and other benefits, some may not be of value to you. For example, if your spouse works and you and your family can be covered on his/her health insurance, getting health insurance via your job may provide no financial advantage.

In closing, it's enormously important for you to consider where you would like to be in five years personally and professionally. That said, does working as a contract programmer or as a company employee get you where you would like to go?

Until next time, work hard, work smart, and continue to grow.

CAN THE JOB TITLE 'DATA SCIENTIST' RAISE YOUR PAY?

Did you know there was a data scientist summit in May 2011 in Las Vegas? I didn't attend, but can you imagine hundreds of data scientists in a casino at the same time. I wonder if the casino lost money that night.

On a serious note, the conference sounds like it had some fascinating topics, such as data visualization and data shifting. More important for this discussion, however, is that if your job is related to analyzing large volumes of data, data visualization, data mining, statistics, or other related areas, you should know that this job title exists and is growing in popularity.

As data grows, it not only gets more difficult to handle, but it can be of extreme value and produce extreme wealth if it's used correctly. Data can, to a certain degree, be used to predict trends in consumer spending, moves in the stock market, and countless other predictive purposes. Data can also be used to make money directly as a product by selling raw data, compiled data, and preanalyzed data. There are also an enormous number of software tools and hardware devices that have been created to collect, store, manipulate, analyze, and visualize data.

OK, fine, we all know data is growing and gaining in value and importance. Why is this being discussed in a column about IT careers? The reason is there are a large number of great IT jobs associated with the topics previously discussed, and, as an additional kicker, they are gaining in stature and becoming more defined.

As an example of a parallel situation that took place in the database administration world, the role of database administrator (DBA) has long been defined and respected. As a result, those who comfortably and appropriately define themselves in this way have had the ability to receive premium jobs and pay over those who simply defined themselves as database knowledgeable.

With all this said, if your job and skill set are deeply involved in statistical data analysis, data visualization, data mining, data filtering, or other similar endeavors, and you think you can walk the walk, consider personally adopting the data scientist title. It may not bring you fame, but it may help bring you fortune.

Until next time, work hard, work smart, and continue to grow.

MANAGING YOUR CAREER

―――――――――

The columns discussed in this chapter are forward thinking by their nature. My hope is that the topics discussed will provide you with insights that will help you navigate the short-term and long-term steps in your professional journey.

These column topics could be best described as one of two types: strategic or tactical. The strategic columns, such as "Proactively manage your career," discuss your career from a holistic and long-term perspective. The tactical topics, such as "Six great social media jobs within IT," are more immediate in regard to where great jobs can be found and what you can do next.

The column "An MBA or a master's in computer science? It's your call" came about from a reader's question. He said that he had finished his undergraduate degree a couple of years ago and was trying to decide what type of master's degree would be of the most value to him professionally. The question really resonated with me personally because I too had to make this decision. For me, I decided on the MBA because I wanted to eventually move into the IT management ranks, even though I loved being a hands-on techie. The answer for you, however, may be very different based on your desired future.

This column, month in and month out, continues to be one of my most heavily read topics. I believe the reason for its continued popularity is threefold.

- First is the massive amount of work, time, and money that will be spent based on the answer to this question. Therefore, people are trying to use the proper due diligence before deciding which direction to go.
- Second, and much more fundamental, people are trying to figure out in the long term which degree will be of most value to them professionally.
- Lastly, this decision to get an MBA or MS in computer science is forcing the employee to answer a much more personal question, "Do I want to stay technical or become a manager?"

How you answer the question "Do I want to stay technical or become a manager?" will help you answer the more immediate question, "An MBA or a master's in computer science?" These two answers will have a very profound impact on your career and your life from that point forward.

If you remember only one thing from this book, let it be the title of this column: "Proactively manage your career." Knowing what you want to do will allow you to formulate a coherent plan to get there. Without a plan, it's easy for years to go by. One day you look up, you're ten years older, and you are no closer to your goal than when you started. Read this column and take it to heart. It could be the difference between meeting your long-term goals and not even knowing what they are.

The column "Eight ways a career coach can help your career" offers a piece of advice I wish I had been given early in my career. I think that it could have made my career a little less bumpy and a little more linear. That said, I truly have great appreciation for those who mentored me or gave me ad hoc advice over the years. It was of great value. As the name of this column alludes, there are many advantages to hiring a professional career coach. The benefits can truly outweigh the financial cost.

The remaining columns in this chapter I would define as tactical, rather than strategic. That is to say, instead of holistically thinking about your long-term career as a whole, the columns in this chapter that are discussed next provide insights and suggestions on your next potential professional step.

The column "Seven questions to ask yourself when selecting an industry for your next job" begin with a very insightful question asked by a reader. Many techies only think about technology being their industry. If the nature of your job is strictly in the internals of IT, such as data security or data communications, then this is for the most part true, but if your job is business-user facing, such as a business analyst or software developer, then your industry experience is equally as important as your technical knowledge and experience. Virtually all business industries can provide great technical careers for techies, but be forewarned that once you pick an industry, over time it will be increasingly more difficult to move in another business direction. The reason for this difficulty is twofold. First, you are more valuable in the industry you know because you understand that industry's data movement, software application types, regulatory issues, and idiosyncrasies. Second, hiring managers, even in IT, generally prefer hiring people with specific industry knowledge because the newly hired employee can come up to speed more quickly.

The column "Five great jobs and six great company startup ideas for people with search engine optimization (SEO) skills" outlines that a specific technical skill, in this case SEO, can provide technical growth in the form of employment or entrepreneurship. Yes, this column specifically discusses SEO. That said, if your technical expertise resides in a different technical area, such as PC support, social media, technical training, etc., consider this two-pronged career approach of employment and being your own boss.

The column "Your hobbies can help your career" describes a way that you can combine what you do and what you love. My assumption is that if you are reading this book, you are a techie of some type. That said, one of the beauties of our profession is that by their nature, as a support function, skill sets like ours are needed in virtually every industry, nonprofit, and social-cause-based organization in the world. Therefore, if you love doing technology and we have deep passion for a specific industry or cause, why not combine the two in your daily vocation?

The last column in the chapter, "Six great social media jobs within IT," was originally inspired by a conversation I had with a person who had a small business helping companies market their products and company brand via social media. Typically, she would help these companies create blogs and participate in industry-specific discussion boards and other similar activities. While she loved having her own business, for a number of reasons she decided that she would rather be an employee, rather than self-employed. Like the SEO column previously mentioned, this column is also an example of how an IT-related skill set lets you move from self-employed to employed and vice versa.

Now, enough for my commentary; enjoy the columns.

AN MBA OR A MASTER'S IN COMPUTER SCIENCE? IT'S YOUR CALL.

The question I was asked:

Two years ago I graduated from college with a degree in computer science from a great engineering school. Now that I have a couple of years' work experience under my belt, I want to begin a part-time master's program. Should I get an MBA or a master's in computer science?

My answer:

My answer to you is that it depends on what you want to do professionally long term. My rationale is that rather than looking at an advanced degree as an end in itself, look at it as a means to an end. Namely, first decide your desired professional direction and then tactically decide which advanced degree has a higher potential to get you there.

As an example, if you would like to move into the IT management ranks, an MBA may be a better route because it teaches you about leadership, budgeting, marketing, and other business-/management-related topics. If, however, you would like to continue on a technical path, find a degree program that expands your technical knowledge in an area that excites you, for example, database design, data security, or another specific technical area.

The reason for suggesting that if you go the technical route you should specialize is because, like it or not, we are in a world of specialization. Becoming a true technical specialist in a high-demand technology can give you an enormous advantage in the job market and command higher pay for your specialized skills.

It may sound counterintuitive; I know it was to me. But specializing in an area of ongoing need, such as database administration, enterprise system architecture, and data communications, can actually make it easier to find a job than if you were a generalist with average knowledge in various technologies.

When I decided to get an MBA, I went into it with the idea that having an MBA may not necessarily help me, but not having an advanced degree would hurt me. This may sound like a terrible premise to spend the time and money required to get an advanced degree, and you would be right. That said, I believe it to be true. When looking for a new job, not having an advanced degree puts you at a disadvantage when competing against people with equal experience and an advanced degree. The other side of that coin is, don't expect you will automatically get the job just because you are the one with the degree. You still have to prove yourself.

Let me leave you with one last thought. I'm very glad I earned an MBA. I gained very important knowledge that truly helped me professionally. It also unlocked doors for me that would have been permanently sealed. My MBA, however, only unlocked the door. I, like all others, had to then work very hard to open these unlocked opportunities.

Until next time, work hard, work smart, and continue to grow.

PROACTIVELY MANAGE YOUR CAREER

People early in their career say "If I work hard, one day I'll be a *this*." *This* could be a chief information officer, systems architect, senior programmer, or any other professional goal you desire. Then, one day, years later, you look up from your day-to-day activities and realize one of the following…

1. Wow, I am now a *this* and I love it!
2. Wow, I am now a *this* and I hate it!
3. I have tried my best to be a *this* and can't quite get there, but I have done my best.
4. I'm not a *this* and don't think I'll get there, because I didn't really put together a plan to get there.

If you are early in your professional career, one of the above four scenarios will most likely come true. If you are further along in your career, like me, one of these four scenarios may already be at play.

If you fall into category one, you probably either planned well or were very lucky. If fact, maybe it was a little of both. Congratulations, you are in the minority and should be very proud both of your achievements and of creating a plan that helped you get there.

If you fall into category two, congratulations are still in order. Well done. You have reached a goal in your working career that you fought hard and long to attain. You should appreciate your achievement. The trick for you now is to decide how you can use your past experiences and success to move toward your next goal. Remember, for motivated people, professional growth is a lifelong journey, not a destination.

If you fall into category three, there is satisfaction in knowing that you fought the good fight. Also, I have learned that life is not a race; as stated above, it's a journey. If you think your goal may still be attainable and you still wish to achieve it, rework your plan and continue your efforts. If you think your goal is truly out of your reach, consider setting your sights in a different direction. After all, Colonel Sanders started Kentucky Fried Chicken in his sixties.

If you fall into category four, know that it's never too late to begin planning. Assess your skills, your successes, and your desires and move forward.

Now, back to those early in their careers. If you truly know what you would like to be ten or twenty years from now, good for you, because many people don't know. If you don't know or haven't seriously thought about it, it could be of great value professionally for you to do some soul searching and introspection as to what you think you would like to do.

All that said, just knowing what you want to be isn't enough. As the saying goes, hope is not an action plan. Do your research, find a mentor, investigate potential future options, assess your skills, and create a plan to get to your desired goal.

- Will your plan change as time goes forward? Yes.
- Will your goals change as your career progresses? Maybe.
- Will your career go exactly as planned? Most likely not.

Will a plan help you move ahead professionally toward your goal? With good planning, hard work, and a little bit of luck, yes.

Until next time, work hard, work smart, and continue to grow.

EIGHT WAYS A CAREER COACH CAN HELP YOUR CAREER

I want to begin this blog by saying that I am not a career coach. I just think they provide great value.

I'm writing on this topic because there were times throughout my career when I think a career coach could have made my professional journey a little easier, a little less complicated, and maybe even a little more lucrative.

I believe that having a paid career coach on your side can be of great value to you professionally in a number of ways, because a coach:

1. can help you bring clarity to your professional goals and aspirations;//
2. doesn't tell you what to do, but rather helps you formulate a plan that fits your needs by asking you questions and then helping you listen to your own answers;
3. gives you an opportunity to talk through the pros and cons of important career decisions with a truly objective and independent person;
4. can steer you toward resources that can help you professionally;

5. is trained in techniques that help you focus on what is most important to you as you move forward in your career;
6. can help you work though difficult career challenges and roadblocks;
7. can help you improve your professional performance by helping you discover blind spots in your work life that can be holding you back professionally;
8. can help you make decisions regarding work/life balance based on your beliefs and priorities.

Having a career coach is not only of value to you, it can also be of value to your employer. Think of it this way: having an independent voice helping you work though problems in the office, by design, is helping you solve problems at your place of business. Remember, at the end of the day, unless you own your own company, the decisions you make and the actions you take at work affect your employer. Also, if having a career coach

- improves your productivity,
- helps you grow professionally,
- enhances your motivation,
- helps you make better decisions, and
- generally helps you be a better employee,

then you are of greater professional value to your company.

In closing, I'd like to say that simply having a career coach can help you think about and take control of your career. It's too easy to just take new jobs as they come along, more opportunistically than thoughtfully. Then one day you look up and realize that ten or fifteen years have gone by and you are virtually no closer to your original professional goals than you were so many years ago. Having someone to help you clarify your professional passion, help you devise a plan to get there, help you work though the inevitable problems along the way, and act as an accountability partner when needed can help you reach your professional aspirations. A career coach, by definition, provides this service.

Until next time, work hard, work smart, and continue to grow.

SEVEN QUESTIONS TO ASK YOURSELF WHEN SELECTING AN INDUSTRY FOR YOUR NEXT JOB

The question I was asked:

I'm a Java developer, was recently laid off, and am now in the process of looking for a new job. Is there a specific industry, such as retail, that you would suggest I concentrate on?

My answer:

As IT professionals, we belong to one of the few professions that can work in almost any industry. I'm sure I'm not surprising you by saying that there are IT people working in health care, financial services, biotech, retail, construction, manufacturing, and about every other industry you can think of.

OK, now to your question, the answer is it depends. When trying to choose the best industry for you to work in, ask yourself the following questions:

1. Do I have any non-IT experience in a specific industry?

This experience could be of value because you will understand the software applications you are building from the user/business perspective.

2. Do I have any educational credential, such as a biology degree or a stockbroker's license, that relates to a specific industry?

Professional business-related credentials in your industry not only provide you with knowledge of the applications you are building, but it also helps give you professional credibility with those on the business side of your company.

3. Is there a specific industry that is predominant in my geographical area?

This is important information for you to know because it relates directly to your future marketability where you live. What you will find as your career progresses and you move to more senior positions is that it gets harder and harder to switch industries. For example, because my technical background is primarily financial services, I am much more professionally marketable within financial services than I am in, say, biotech or retail.

4. Is there an industry I like the most?

My point here is that if there is an industry you really love, you might as well work in an industry that you find interesting.

5. Is there an industry where I have close, highly placed connections?

Very often in business, it's not only what you know, but who you know. Having personal connections in your industry can be very valuable to you professionally.

6. Is there an industry where the software applications I have worked on in the past are in high demand?

Depending on how long you have been professionally employed, the applications you have been working on in the past may be valued more in some industries than others. For example, if you have deep software development experience building patient billing systems for a hospital, this specialized experience will be most valued by the health care industry, somewhat valued within financial services, and less valued within manufacturing and biotech.

7. Is there an industry that my skills are particularly suited for?

I know that you are a Java programmer, but beyond that, if your technical skills lean toward a specific area, such as mobile devices, real-time systems, website development, etc., these specific skills are more heavily valued and used in some industries more than others.

In closing, at the end of the day, any industry can provide you with a great professional IT career. The trick is to find an industry that you like, where your skills and strengths are appreciated, and where you are fairly compensated.

If this is of value to you, I personally have two undergraduate degrees, one in accounting and one in computer systems. Professionally, I have spent the majority of my professional career working in IT within the financial services industry, and always on accounting and financial-related systems. Over the years, even within the IT function, my background in accounting has been of great value to me because I was able to understand the business purpose of the software applications I was building.

Until next time, work hard, work smart, and continue to grow.

FIVE GREAT JOBS AND SIX GREAT COMPANY STARTUP IDEAS FOR PEOPLE WITH SEARCH ENGINE OPTIMIZATION (SEO) SKILLS

There are some technical specialties that not only provide great employment opportunities, but also create the possibility of using them to start your own business. Search engine optimization (SEO) is one of these skill sets.

Potential jobs for people with SEO skills include:

1. Working internally for a company whose business model depends on high organic search results.

2. Working for a web design company to help assure that the websites it creates are technically structured in a way that maximizes search engine visibility.

3. Working for a company that provides SEO as a service.

4. Working for a company heavily involved in social media to assure their blog posts contain the right mix of key search words to help maximize search engine visibility.

5. Working for a marketing type company heavily involved in social media to help assure the maximum search value of their marketing campaigns and social-media-based outreach.

From an entrepreneurial perspective, SEO skills provide you the following possibilities:

1. Become a professional speaker on how people can optimize their websites for maximum visibilities.

2. Start a company that consults with clients on how to optimize their websites.

3. Start a company that provides ongoing SEO services for clients (often combined with item two above).

4. Start a training business teaching people how SEO works and specific things they can do to optimize their websites.

5. If you are a software developer by background, consider creating and selling an SEO-oriented software product and/or cloud-based service.

6. If you like to write, create a business writing SEO-efficient blog posts for client companies.

If SEO is an area where you would like to work or start a company, please note that while it is a thriving industry, there is also an ever-growing amount of competition. That said, I would consider trying to build your personal reputation and personal brand. The idea is that as you become better known as an SEO subject matter expert, it will be easier for you to find employment and/or successfully start your own company. In fact, since you know SEO, use it to your advantage to help create your reputation and brand. This is a double win for you. First, and most obvious, your SEO skills will help you be seen by others. Second, you can be your own first client. That is to say, once you are successful publicizing yourself, you can use your personal SEO success as a case study as to how you can help others.

Until next time, work hard, work smart, and continue to grow.

YOUR HOBBIES CAN HELP YOUR CAREER

───────────────

Are you a techie by day and a dancer by night? How about a writer, football coach, musician, or car repair enthusiast? If so, this column is for you.

One thing that's great about being a professional techie is that virtually every business, government organization, nonprofit group, religious order, and professional association needs your knowledge and expertise. This ability to potentially work for any company anywhere in the country or worldwide has two huge advantages.

- You have the ability to work for any type of organization.
- Knowledge of your hobby brings you added marketability to that industry.

Regarding your ability to work at any organization, this allows you to try to find an organization that does work that you believe in. For example, if you believe in the importance of clean energy, try to find an IT job at a company that manufactures windmills, solar panels, or other renewable energy products. This can be a double win for you. Not only will you be working with people who are like-minded, you will also be helping forward a cause you believe in.

Regarding your hobby-based knowledge, if your hobby or interest brings with it a large or specialized body of knowledge and/or experience, you may be very personally marketable to the IT groups and software vendors that support that industry. For example, if you are a data mining professional, love football, and pride yourself on being an expert in NFL player and team statistics, try to get a job working for a team in the NFL as a statistician. You may already be more qualified for the position than you think.

The idea here is that the combination of your computer skill, passion for the topic, and deep personal knowledge of the subject makes you uniquely qualified for a job in an area you really love.

A real-life example of combining technical expertise and personal passion was exhibited on the TV show *America's Got Talent*. Miral Kotb, from the dance group named iLuminate, was a software engineer with a passion for dance. She was a dancer who conquered a personal struggle with cancer that reduced her physical ability to dance. She then combined her technical knowledge of software engineering with her passion for dance and masterminded a light-based dance team that reached the finals. This combination of technology and great dance choreography was fabulous to watch and almost won the group a million dollars and a show in Las Vegas.

This type of story could be you, if you can find a way to combine what you know with what you love.

Until next time, work hard, work smart, and continue to grow.

SIX GREAT SOCIAL MEDIA JOBS WITHIN IT

The question I was asked:

Are there any social-media-related jobs within a traditional IT group?

My answer:

Hello, Chris, and thanks for your e-mail. Yes, there are various types of social media jobs within IT. These job types loosely fall into the following categories:

1. Website interaction

2. Customer interaction

3. Active listening

4. New employee investigation

5. Internal employee interaction

6. Training augmentation

1. Website interaction: User/website interaction is not always considered a form of social media, but I like to think of it as one. I think this way because aspects of many company websites are designed to be interactive with their customers. Once in place, your customers can interact with your company without human employee interaction. Examples of this automated interaction include the download of white papers, access to various types of information, and the purchase of online products. All of these activities bring your customers closer to your company, which, in fact, is one of the goals of corporate-based social media. From a job perspective, all of these user/website interactions need to be initially built and maintained on an ongoing basis by IT staff members.

2. Customer interaction: Company marketing and public relations departments directly interact with the public via blogs, Twitter, LinkedIn, Facebook, and other communication mediums. In addition to these communication mediums, there is also a growing number of third-party products that help facilitate the use of Twitter, LinkedIn, Facebook, and others. From a job perspective, these departments generally need internal IT support to help set up and manage the technical aspects of these social media tools.

3. Active listening: Active listening is an extremely important and lesser-known social media activity. Active listening is the art and science of collecting, analyzing, and reporting all of the web-based chat and comments made about your company, its products, and its competitors.

This information is used by internal marketing, product development, customer service, sales, and strategic planning to maximize the company's products, customer service, and general competitive edge. These activities require software monitoring tools such as Maestro and Visible Intelligence. From a job perspective, the implementation of these tools and the collection, storage, and distribution of information that is collected require IT staff members on an ongoing basis.

4, New employee investigation: If you didn't know this yet, you should. Human resources (HR) and recruiting organizations are now doing web-based and social-media-based searches and analysis on people they are considering hiring. In many cases, the HR groups need internal IT support to conduct these activities.

5. Internal employee interaction: Companies also use social media tools like wikis and blogs internally to facilitate the communication of best practices, company success stories, project status, and other types of information. Some people also include software such as Microsoft SharePoint and Lotus Notes as tools used within this category. From a job perspective, all of these internal products and activities require some level of IT support.

6. Training augmentation: Best practices in the training world now incorporate social media tools such as wikis, blogs, and discussion boards as a way of maximizing training effectiveness by facilitating the interaction among students and between students and their instructors. From a job perspective, the software used to facilitate this communication generally requires IT involvement.

In closing, throughout this column, I have continually mentioned the need for IT support and involvement. This support means you. I also believe that as time moves forward, the demand for these types of jobs will continue to increase.

Until next time, work hard, work smart, and continue to grow.

CAREER ADVANCEMENT TIPS AND ADVICE

This chapter contains a collection of columns related to personal growth and/or change within the workplace. The reason these two types of columns are together is because in many ways, they are two sides of the same coin. That is to say, professional growth very often requires personal change, and when changes occur in the workplace, survival often requires personal growth.

That said, the first three columns in this section deal with different aspects of professional growth and the personal implications related to these career moves. The last two columns discuss change in the workplace: one due to IT's movement toward cloud computing and the other related to organizational change in general.

The first column, "Helpdesk support technician wants more," was inspired by a reader who has the potential for career advancement if he moves to a job on the second shift. For those not familiar with the term "second shift," it refers to the time of day that you are working. "First shift" refers to standard business hours. "Second shift" is generally from approximately 4:00 p.m. to midnight.

The key takeaway from this column is that sometimes professional growth comes with some type of personal sacrifice for you and/or your family. It may be working second shift or it may be moving to a new city. Each time these situations arise, you must analyze the opportunity from all possible perspectives, including the following:

- Will the job help you meet your long-term goals?
- Can you do the job well?
- What impact will the new job have on your family life and work/life balance?
- Is it a job that you will be happy doing?

The column "Programmer seeks advice on how to become a manager" was one of my original columns and, as a result, is in the shorter format. That said, it just touches the surface as to the things you can do to prepare and position yourself to be a manager. In fact, this topic alone could be its own book, and actually is. Many of the tips listed below are explained in detail within my *Manager Mechanics: Tips and Advice for First-Time Managers* and expanded upon within my *52 Great Management Tips* books. They are also discussed in detail within various "Manager Mechanics" classroom-based and e-learning-based classes.

That said, at a high level, here are some things to consider if you would like to eventually move into a management role:

- Make sure that you want to be a manager. Managing the work is very different than doing the work.
- Throughout your career, you should learn from the managers around you. Watch them closely and see what they do right, as well as what they do wrong.
- If possible, try to learn more about the processes performed within your department by cross training on other department jobs.
- Gain an understanding of key applications supported by IT.
- Gain an understanding of companywide data movement.

- Gain an understanding of IT-based standards and methodologies.
- Learn more about your IT group's primary hardware and software vendors.
- Learn more about the third-party products in your technical area and business industry.
- Read the job description of the position you would like next and use it as the basis for an action plan to get there.
- Work to enhance your professional certifications and education level.
- Attend any internal company training classes that you believe will help you move forward.
- Practice being a manager by volunteering for cross-department committees and/or leadership positions at your favorite civic, charitable, or religious organization.

Take the column "Seven places to step outside your comfort zone and get promoted" to heart. Stepping outside your comfort zone isn't an easy thing to do. I know, I've done it and continue to do it because I still want to grow as a person and a professional. My hope is that you do also. As you will see when reading the column, you will be asked to take on personal challenges to move forward with your career. These challenges will be different for everyone, but everyone will have something. It may be giving presentations. It may be learning a new type of technology. It may be working with those less technical than you, but you will be challenged by some aspect of your job. Your ability to succeed will be based on your ability to move forward even when it's personally difficult to do so.

The last two columns in this chapter deal with change. As most people in the workforce can attest, it seems that the only constant in business is change. As a result, the greater your ability to accept and adapt to change in your department, your company, and your industry, the greater chance you will have to be successful within your profession.

The column "Cloud computing can help or hurt your career" was inspired by a question from a reader who was worried about his job and future at the company because of rumors that the CIO was moving toward the use of cloud computing with the company's IT shop. As you shall read, all change has the potential to bring risks and stress along with it. On the positive side, it can also bring great rewards for those who embrace the change and use it to their strategic advantage.

The last column in this chapter, "Change is a four-letter word: "gold," and six great ways to get some," expands on this theme that while stressful and risky, with a little bit of luck and the right attitude, change within the workplace can dramatically help you professionally.

Now, enough for my commentary; enjoy the columns.

CLOUD COMPUTING CAN HELP OR HURT YOUR CAREER

The question I was asked:

It has been rumored that our IT organization is considering using cloud-based technologies inside and outside the company. Is this good or bad for me?

My answer:

As many people say, the only constant in business is change. I truly believe this is true not only for business, but for IT and the technologies that drive it. I'm of the opinion that IT-related technologies have a half-life of two years. That is to say, the skill set and knowledge you have today will be only half as marketable two years from now because:

- new hardware and software versions are released, which reduces your currency in the technology;
- as technologies become more established, the competitive edge for those who know it are reduced because the technology is more well known;
- the introduction of new, innovative technologies can quickly marginalize older technologies and quickly make them obsolete;

- companies begin chasing newer technologies if they believe it makes good business sense.

Cloud computing is one of those technologies that is truly taking the computer industry by storm. In fact, many refer to cloud computing as a megatrend, like the introduction of PCs, client-server computing, and the creation of the Internet. Indications are that cloud computing is truly a trend of this magnitude.

Like all big trends in the computer industry, including those previously mentioned, there are winners and losers. That said, cloud computing has the potential to revitalize our industry. It has the potential to push some techies aside and, for those who come aboard, bring others on the ride of their professional life.

Let's begin with the downside of cloud computing from a career perspective. If the internal software you are supporting is moved to the cloud, it's possible you will lose your job. This can be very ugly in today's economy. This is the case because, in essence, this type of cloud computing is a type of outsourcing, which is the fear of many professions.

On the lighter side, IT cloud-computing-based initiatives have the potential to:

- expand your skill set;
- change your IT group from a cost center into a revenue producer if your internally created cloud-based applications are sold externally by the company;
- expand the role of business analysts because companies are able to implement software applications that would have otherwise been too expensive to implement;
- spawn large new IT initiatives with the goal of rewriting and/or retrofitting existing software applications to work within internally created private cloud environments.

There have also been a large number of self-funded and venture-capital-backed software companies that need techies of all kinds to build their cloud-computing-based products.

As an IT professional, it would absolutely be worth your while to learn about the aspects of cloud computing that touch your specific professional area. If you are a software developer, learn to program it. If you are a tester, learn how to test it. If you are an IT manager, learn how to manage it.

Like it or not, cloud computing is a megatrend within our industry. Those who can make it dance have the opportunity to profit from it.

Until next time, work hard, work smart, and continue to grow.

HELPDESK SUPPORT TECHNICIAN WANTS MORE

The question I was asked:

I have worked for the last two years as a help desk support technician. I have a good reputation with the people I help and like the work. The thing is, I'm getting really bored. A job at the company opened for a second-shift operator in the data center. Do you think I should take it?

My answer:

Let me begin by asking you two questions. First, what job would you like to have in five years? Second, what effect would working second shift have on your family and work/life balance?

The reason I asked you these two questions is because their answers play a significant role in my advice to you. If you know where you would like to be professionally in five years, then you will be in a position to decide if a second-shift job in the data center would help you get there. If your answer is no, then your decision is made. If your answer is yes, it's moving you in the direction you would like to go, then my second question becomes relevant, namely, what effect will working second shift have on your personal life.

My assumption is that second shift at your company is 4:00 p.m. to midnight. Some people love this shift; other people never get used to it and dream of the day they can go back to standard working hours.

The moral of the story is that when considering a new job, don't look at the job in isolation. Make sure you are taking it for the right reasons and that once the novelty wears off, you can live with the day-to-day ramifications of your decision.

Until next time, work hard, work smart, and continue to grow.

PROGRAMMER SEEKS ADVICE ON HOW TO BECOME A MANAGER

The question I was asked:

I have been working as a programmer for about five years. I would like to move to a manager job. How do I make the jump from individual contributor to manager?

My answer:

There are a number of things that you can do to begin positioning yourself for a manager's job. These include cross training on other department applications, volunteering for cross-department projects, taking a leadership role on internal department activities, gaining an understanding of important department processes, and beginning to act like a manager.

This may seem like a lot to do, but each of these items will help you in a different way. Cross-training will widen your knowledge of internal company applications. Being involved in cross-department initiatives gives you exposure to people outside your department and may give you a taste of manager-level politics. Taking a leadership role on small internal projects allows you to practice your management craft while simultaneously showcasing your leadership abilities to those in a position to promote you. Gaining an understanding of departmentwide processes will give you a wider perspective on the business of software development. Lastly, act like a manager, by which I mean dressing appropriately, mentoring junior staff members, meeting project deadlines, and other similar activities.

As a final thought, analyze whether you have the appropriate credentials to move to a management role. In particular, does your company require the completion of an internal management training program, an advanced college degree, and/or an industry-specific certification to be eligible for a management position?

CHANGE IS A FOUR-LETTER WORD: "GOLD," AND SIX GREAT WAYS TO GET SOME

Wow, what an industry we're in, megatrend after megatrend: cloud computing, tablet computers, GPS-enabled devices, smartphones, not-so-smartphones, and more. There's gold in them there trends for the techies that can identify a unique niche, application type, business need, or job opportunity.

These industry-changing trends can be of great career and financial benefit to you. Consider the following:

1. Do your research and find job openings at companies that you think will grow dramatically because of current industry trends and changes. All ships rise in high tide. If you work for a growing company, chances are that you can grow with it; not to mention the potential value of stock options and/or stock purchase plans if available.

2. If you are at a company you love, try to discover ways that your company can take advantage of new and evolving technologies. This has two advantages for you: first, it can help you become an internal company thought leader; second, using these technologies will enhance your personal/professional marketability.

3. If your company is moving toward new technologies, such as developing an internal company private cloud, try to get involved. It can help establish your role as a participant in the company's new technical direction. Also, if your company's plan is to replace older technologies with newer ones, working on these newer technologies could save your job.

4. If you are entrepreneurial by nature, your skill set is aligned with one of these new technologies, and your personal situation allows it, now may be the time to try to start your own company on a part-time or full-time basis.

5. If you are in an internal IT group, try to align new technologies with the business needs of the groups you support. If you can do it cost effectively, you can provide real value to your business users, IT, and your company in general.

6. If you like to write or speak at conferences as a way of enhancing your professional brand, experience and practical knowledge in an up-and-coming technology can help you get published and/or a speaking slot at a professional conference.

As mentioned in earlier columns, industry-changing trends like cloud computing have the potential to generate winners and losers because of their technology shift. Other technologies, such as tablet computing, smartphones, and GPS-enabled devices, because they are new technology paradigms, tend to bring immense opportunities with minimum short-term risk to other technologies because they are an "addition to" rather than a "replacement of" type product. In the longer term, however, these "addition to" technologies will, in fact, reduce the demand for other products. For example, fewer people today buy paper maps because their cars have GPS systems.

This change in buying patterns, however, has taken years to take form.

In closing, how many people do you think have said to themselves or others, "Wow, I wish I had gotten involved in the Internet when it first became popular"? (I'm not actually looking for a specific number; this question was just rhetorical. J)

Well, five or ten years from now, don't be the one saying the same thing about today's new technologies. Learn about them and get involved. If you do, the combination of hard work, backing the right horse, and more than a little good luck may bring your wealth and professional growth.

Until next time, work hard, work smart, and continue to grow.

SEVEN PLACES TO STEP OUTSIDE YOUR COMFORT ZONE AND GET PROMOTED

Sometimes the things we want to do the least are exactly the things we need to do to get promoted. The issue is that there are many times in our lives, both personal and professional, that personal advancement requires personal growth.

In some cases, personal growth is in the areas we love to pursue. For example, if you love playing tennis and want to become a nationally rated player, you have to practice, and maybe take lessons, to improve your game. If you love playing tennis, then personal growth in this area is welcomed and anticipated. As a counterexample, if getting promoted requires learning to successfully manage projects, but delegating work to others is difficult for you, you have an issue. It doesn't mean you can't do it, it just means that you must step outside your comfort zone to acquire the skill.

As techies, or for that matter as human beings, there are a number of areas, both personal and professional, in which we may not naturally be comfortable. Some of these items that follow may be on your list.

Learning technologies you don't currently know: This one may sound funny for a techie, but it's very common. Maybe you are a

COBOL programmer and would like to update your skills, but the needed body of knowledge seems too large to undertake.

Giving a presentation: For many people, the thought of standing up in front of the room and giving a presentation, particularly if their boss is listening, is petrifying and seems like a fate worse than death.

Leading a project: Leading a project requires taking risk, taking responsibly, delegating work to others, setting objectives, and meeting deadlines.

Writing documentation: Many software developers hate to write documentation. Programming environments don't have spell checkers. Maybe English is your second language. Many programmers believe that if you can't read and understand the source code, you shouldn't be trying to modify the software; therefore, documentation within the code has no value. Maybe for some people these are nothing more than reasons to not write documentation, because they do not feel comfortable doing it.

Training users: Training users on how to use the software you have written may feel frustrating and/or scary. First, training is like giving a presentation, and we already talked about that one. Second, what if the users don't like the software you created? Then what?

Cross training other programmers to do your job: This may just seem wrong. It's your job, why should you teach someone else to do it? Additionally, you have too much work to do to spend the time.

Learning the nightly production cycle: Wow, there is so much to learn. What if you're on call one night and can't fix the problem? You will have to call people in the middle of the night and wake them up.

When reading this list, some of the items may resonate with you, while others may seem funny or contrived. Truth be told, I have seen all these objections over the years, and at the end of the day, these objections were primarily based on fear and/or discomfort by the objector, rather than on objective considerations. Additionally, all of these items hindered the professional growth of their owner. The takeaway here for you is to sit back and think about what comfort zones you must move beyond to grow as a person and a professional.

Until next time, work hard, work smart, and continue to grow.

BUILDING YOUR PROFESSIONAL/TECHNICAL BRAND

In many ways, this chapter is very different from the previous chapters. The first two chapters in the book discussed ways to enhance your skill sets, both technical and nontechnical. The third chapter provided tips on how to find a new job. The next chapter, "In the Workplace," provided various insights related to surviving and flourishing within your office environment. From there, the book provided insights on ways to maximize your pay, manage your career, and tips and advice on how to move ahead professionally.

This chapter, by contrast, is not about you, the person; it's about you, the product. This may sound very impersonal, and, well, it is. This chapter is not about what you know or what you think of yourself. This chapter is about what others think you know and what others think of you. Therefore, when reading this chapter, the more you can detach yourself from you, the person, and look at yourself from the outside looking in, the more you will understand the subtleties of the topics within this chapter.

In essence, this chapter provides insights into how to market yourself to others. Following on the "you are the product" theme mentioned earlier, let's contrast sales and marketing. Sales (of you) are when you find potential employers and call them, e-mail them, or send them your resume. That is to say, you are contacting them. Marketing (of you) is when you make yourself known in the marketplace by blogging, speaking at conferences, participating in discussion boards, and other proactive activities that help others find you.

The first column in this chapter, "Six great social media tips for techies," was inspired by a reader interested in using social media, not because of its technical attributes, but how he, as a techie, can use social media to expand his personal brand. We as techies have a huge advantage over our nontechnical counterparts when it comes to using social media on our own behalf. We understand and are not afraid of technology. The lesson here is, as a technologist, use technology to expand your personal brand and enhance your professional future.

If done correctly, attending a technical conference can expand your knowledge, increase your professional contacts, and enhance your personal brand. If not done correctly, you simply get a couple of days out of the office, a T-shirt or two for yourself, and a few trinkets for your kids.

The column "Value of technical conferences" describes ways to take full advantage of your time spent at technical conferences and how you maximize their value to both your employer and yourself personally.

The column "Value of IT certifications" was in response to a very specific question from a reader I believe was rather skeptical about the value of technical certifications. When you read this column, consider it from two perspectives: first, from the perspective of a techie trying to decide if he/she should begin studying for technical certification, and second, from the perspective of a hiring manager. In this second case, all other things being equal (professional experience, department fit, etc.), which person would you hire if you could only hire one person?

Next, ask yourself a theoretical question: What if the governing body of a well-known certification called you and said that he/she thought you were so smart that you could simply have the certification? Additionally, let's say it was a prestigious certification, such as a PMP or CISCO certification. Ethical issues aside, would you accept it, and do you think it would be of value to you professionally? If you said yes, then the question is not the certification's value, it's the level of effort to attain it, versus the professional value it will provide.

I love the column "Helping build open-source software can help your career," not because of its wit and wisdom, but because it provides a way for techies to do something good for the world, good for the technology community, and good for themselves all at the same time. If you are looking for a way to expand your technical skills, learn new things, meet new people, expand your personal brand, and do something good for the world, get involved and participate in an open-source project that you find of interest and of value. I have found that when I have offered to provide my help to others with the goal of truly just helping them, some way and somehow my actions have always seemed to be of value to me. I wish you the same experience.

The column "Top ten reasons to get a PMP certification, even if you're a seasoned pro" has been one of my most popular columns over time. It raises an interesting question, not only for project managers, but for all seasoned/experienced technical professionals. This question is, "When has my professional experience and expertise outreached the value of an industry-recognized certification?" When reading this column, as a project manager or otherwise, remember to try to consider it from the other people's perspective of you, rather than your perspective of yourself.

The column "I want to work in a project management office (PMO)" is an example of how building your personal brand in a specific direction and with a specific purpose can help you reach a specific goal. As you will read, a business analyst e-mailed me a question asking how she can gain employment within a PMO. In short, this column outlines a strategy that suggests she expand her knowledge (improve herself) and find places within the company to showcase this knowledge (building her brand).

The last column in this chapter, "Building your personal brand," now holds few mysteries regarding the definition, creation, or expansion of your professional brand. That said, it will reinforce some of the key points that have been addressed within this chapter's introduction.

As a closing thought to you on this topic before reading the columns within, many people find it difficult to talk about themselves. It feels like bragging and self-indulgence. Truth be told, I feel that way and like to think of it as self-promotion and a necessary evil to move ahead professionally. If, like me, you find this a little uncomfortable, please recall and reread the column "Seven places to step outside your comfort zone and get promoted," not in regard to the seven items listed, but in regard to reaching outside your comfort zone. I know it's difficult for me, and I believe it is also difficult for most others.

Now, enough for my commentary; enjoy the columns.

SIX GREAT SOCIAL MEDIA TIPS FOR TECHIES

The question I was asked:

I'm an independent web developer specializing in Java, PHP, and MySQL. How can I use social media to build my personal brand?

My answer:

As a techie, whether you are working independently or employed by a company, social media can help you professionally in a number of ways, including the following:

- Becoming known as a thought leader in your technical area
- Making contacts that can help you sell your services and/or find a job
- Enhancing/expanding your technical knowledge via online dialogue with other techies
- Getting assistance technically by posting questions on technology-oriented discussion boards

There are a number of things that you can do to help realize these advantages. They are:

- Answer questions listed on technical discussion boards. This helps you showcase your technical ability and your willingness to provide value as part of the online community.

- Concentrate all of your social media activities within a single technical area. As counterintuitive as it sounds, it's easier to get work as a specialist than it is as a generalist. This is the case because in a competitive market, people look for the best person they can find in a given technology. This puts a specialist over a generalist almost every time.
- Tweet insightful technical ideas in your area of concentrated specialty. These tweets should be related to questions you answered on the technical discussion boards. Writing this material takes time. Therefore, with this technique of write then tweet, you get double benefit.
- If it's still available, get your name as a website domain. For example, in addition to my company's URL, **www.ManagerMechanics.com**, I also have the URL of my name. If your name is taken, don't be discouraged, be creative. My first and last name was taken. Apparently the name Eric Bloom is also rather musical (except, of course, for me), because the lead singer of a rock band I loved as a kid, Blue Oyster Cult, is also named Eric Bloom. Therefore, I added my middle initial and the URL **www.EricPBloom**.com was born. Use this website to showcase your technical knowledge. This will further connect your name with your area of technical concentration.
- Write a blog, again concentrating on your chosen technical specialty. Within this blog, however, feel free to discuss other technical topics that relate to your technical specialty. This widened discussion within your blog will help show your versatility and, in time, may potentially allow you to expand your repertoire.
- Follow and retweet technical tweets you like from other people within your technical concentration. This will add to your reputation as a thought leader, help you develop

a personal network of like-minded professionals, and, with luck, they will begin retweeting your tweets as a thank you.

In closing, I just want to say that while social media is a great way to grow your personal/professional brand, don't ignore the incredible value of face-to-face discussions with like-minded people at professional associations, technical conferences, and other professionally minded organizations. The combination of face to face and PC to PC (social media) can be an unbeatable.

Until next time, work hard, work smart, and continue to grow.

VALUE OF TECHNICAL CONFERENCES

Cool locations aside, with proper planning, a technical conference can be of real value to you and your company.

This planning is divided into two parts: picking the right conference, and budgeting your time once there.

Don't technical conferences sound like fun? At their best, you get whisked off to cool locations like Las Vegas and New Orleans. At their worst, they are down the street from where you work and you have to come back to the office in time for a 4:00 staff meeting.

Regarding picking the right conference, consider the following:

- Do you think the keynote speakers provide you insights that will help you at work as well as help you grow professionally?
- Will you immediately be using the technologies you will be learning at the conference? If not, the knowledge you have gained will fade by the time you need to use it.
- Will there be the opportunity for professional networking? If yes, is it with people that can be of value to you professionally?
- Given that all companies have limited budgets, is this the best conference for you to go to from your company's and your professional perspective?

- Is the conference at a time that will not adversely affect your current work projects and/or deliverables?
- Is the conference at a time that will not adversely affect your family beyond standard traveling inconveniences?

As you can see, the nature of these questions is to try to assure that the conference has the dual value of being good for the company and good for you. After all, it's your company's money and your time.

Now that you have decided which conference to attend, the second part of your planning is the development of a plan to get as much as you can out of the conference. Remember, even though a technical conference may have an element of fun, it's still work and should be treated as such. That said, your preconference planning should include the following items:

If there are simultaneous sessions, carefully decide which sessions to attend. Review the list of exhibitors/vendors and write out a list of which vendors you want to visit.

If a list of attendees is available, review the list for former coworkers you would like to reconnect with and companies where you would like to develop a contact.

Try to book your hotel room in the same hotel as the conference. It will save you time and make the logistics much simpler.

Book your plane flights early to save your company money. Also, if your plane tickets are already purchased, it's less likely that your boss will change his/her mind and not let you attend, particularly if the tickets are nonrefundable.

Ask your boss and co-workers what information they would like you to bring back from the conference. This increases the value of the conference to your company.

Once at the conference consider the following:

When you pack to go to the conference, leave room in your suitcase for the stuff you will want to bring home from the conference (books you won't read, T-shirts you will never wear, free toys your kids won't like, etc.).

If two sessions you would like to attend are held at the same time, whichever one you go to, sit in the back; that way, if it's not very good you can sneak out and go to the other session. If you are sitting in the front or in the middle of a line of chairs, it is much harder to quietly and politely exit.

Talk to as many people as you can. It's always good to expand your professional network. Also, if you can make a good contact with one of your company's vendors or clients, it can be of great value to your company.

When walking through the vendor area, the exhibitors with the biggest lines have either the best technologies or the best giveaway toys. Visiting this exhibitor is either a win for you or a win for your kids.

If the session you are in is really boring and of no value to you, sneak out, go to the exhibit hall, and visit the vendors you have on your "must-see" list. The vendors are far less busy when the sessions are in progress and will be able to give you more time.

If most of the vendors are giving away candy, don't eat too much of it. It's not good for you and will make you sick if you don't pay attention to how much you are eating. Please note that on this item in particular, far too often I have not followed my own advice. :)

In closing, if you are going to the conference anyway, get everything you can out of it. After all, both your company's money and your time are bad things to waste.

Until next time, work hard, work smart, and continue to grow

VALUE OF IT CERTIFICATIONS

The question I was asked:

What is the real value of the various IT-related certifications? Is it worth my time and money to get one?

My answer:

The short answer to your question is yes, an IT-oriented certification can be of great value to you if it's in an area that you are trying to pursue professionally.

IT-based certifications have long been a mainstay of IT education and professional credentials. It's been my experience that these certifications have two main advantages. First, and most important, they provide a framework by which technical people can learn and gain a level of proficiency in a specific IT-related topic. Second, it provides the recipient with a credential showing he/she has a defined body of knowledge in a specific area.

When I was an IT manager trying to hire new people, I looked at IT-related certifications from the perspective that if the person cares enough about his/her career to spend his/her time and money

- pursuing knowledge and credentials in a specialized area of technical study,
- finding and signing up for classes,

- studying for an exam, and
- passing an exam,

then this person is

- a self-starter,
- follows through on planned activities,
- is professionally minded,
- and has knowledge in a defined area of study.

All other things being equal, the person with the certification will most likely be the person that I would hire. That said, if things are not equal, which is mostly the case, I would view the certifications as a positive contributing factor in the decision of who to hire.

I have also seen certain IT organizations that require, or highly prefer, a specified certification such as ITIL or Six Sigma if the company is in the process of rolling out these methodologies throughout their organizations. In this case, if you have one of these certifications, you are in an excellent position to get hired.

There are a number of great IT-oriented certifications that may be of value to you, based on your current professional knowledge and/or your future career aspirations. They are:

- PMP—if you are or would like to be a project manager
- ITIL—Information Technology Infrastructure Library
- ITMLP and ITMLE—if you would like to become an IT manager
- Lean Six Sigma—methodology that uses data and statistical analysis
- Cisco CCNA—Cisco Certified Network Associate
- MCITP, MCTS, and MCSE—certifications on various Microsoft products

This is by no means a complete list of great industry certificates. It's just a small list of some of the great IT certifications that are out there. My suggestion to you is that if there is a specific area of study that you are trying to professionally pursue, see if there is a certification in that area. If there is, it will not only give you a framework from which to study, but it will also give a professional credential in your area of interest and connect you into the mainstream of thought leadership in your chosen area.

Until next time, work hard, work smart, and continue to grow.

HELPING BUILD OPEN-SOURCE SOFTWARE CAN HELP YOUR CAREER

Some techies become part of open-source communities and develop professional-quality software for free. Then, when the software is production ready, they give it away. This is the nature of open-source systems. Participating in these projects is not only good for the world; it can also be good for you.

I have a friend who is a dentist. After a hard day of filling cavities, cleaning teeth, and doing root canals, I'm pretty sure that when he gets home and wants to relax, he doesn't look in people's mouths for fun.

Many techies, however, after a busy day of writing software, fixing PCs, and so on, go home and do basically the same thing for fun. Some techies

- try to learn new programming languages;
- read technical journals;
- test out new operating system versions;
- assemble computers and other electronic devices from the base components;
- help their friends build websites;
- start companies.

For those who may not be familiar with open-source projects, they include the following incredibly well done, and wildly successful software:

- Linux
- Apache
- MySQL
- PHP
- Moodle
- Open Sim

There are also a number of other really great and worthwhile projects, almost too many to name.

Programmers help develop open-source software for a number of great and selfless reasons, including

- the desire to advance the state of the art of computing;
- the ability to participate in the creation of great software;
- the opportunity to work with some of the best programmers in the world;
- the ability to be truly creative and have an impact.

All of the above are great reasons to become involved in the open-source community. That said, in addition to the pure satisfaction gained from working on these projects, it can also be professionally advantageous and can:

enhance your software development skills;

allow you to meet other developers within the open-source community;

gain a deep, developer-level understanding of commonly used software products;

expand your resume with interesting and impressive new credentials;

learn new programming techniques;

enhance your understanding of large software development project management and control;

make worldwide professional contacts.

I am by no means suggesting that you become actively involved in open-source projects just for the personal professional gain, because this would be inconsistent with the values and true reason that open-source projects and systems exist. That said, should you choose to participate for the right reasons, not only will you gain the satisfaction of doing a good thing for the computer industry in general, but you will be enhancing your own career as well.

Until next time, work hard, work smart, and continue to grow.

TOP TEN REASONS TO GET A PMP CERTIFICATION, EVEN IF YOU'RE A SEASONED PRO

The question I was asked:

I have about ten years experience working as a project manager. Is it worthwhile for me to get my PMP certification, or have I worked long enough that I don't really need it?

My answer:

I'm a strong believer in professional certifications. I think they show professional commitment, a specified level of knowledge, and a presumption of technical expertise.

Regarding your question of whether a PMP is right for you, it depends on what you want to do professionally long term. Getting a PMP is a big investment in both time and money. If you feel that project management has been a good stepping-stone for you and you are ready to move on, then no, it may not be worth your while. That said, if you want to be a project manager long term, then yes, it can have incredible value to you.

The PMP is a great certification and carries with it a high level of prestige within the project management and information technology (IT) community. I would also say that a PMP is highly respected within non-IT communities where strong project management skills are required.

If you plan on a long-term career as a project manager, then yes, even with your level of experience, I would suggest getting your PMP. I say this for the following reasons.

1. It will expose you to mainstream thinking on project management standards, techniques, best practices, and current trends.
2. You will learn great new tricks and techniques to assist you in your project management activities.
3. When hiring, many companies are now giving preference to project managers that are PMP certified.
4. It's a formalized display of your professional ability.
5. If working for a consulting firm, your PMP credential may help your company win business, making you more valuable to your firm.
6. It will provide networking opportunities with other PMPs.
7. It will impress your friends at cocktail parties.
8. It will provide potential teaching opportunities by teaching PMP classes to future PMP candidates
9. It illustrates personal drive to further your credentials, knowledge, and professional abilities.
10. It helps to distinguish you from other project management professionals in this tough job market.

FINDING A JOB IN A PROJECT MANAGEMENT OFFICE (PMO)

―――――――――

The question I was asked:

I'm personally a strong proponent of PMOs, so I'm glad this question came up. If correctly done, a PMO can enhance an IT organization's effectiveness and productivity.

My answer:

For those who are not familiar with PMOs, a PMO is a department within the IT organization that specializes in methodology, documentation, process, and/or project management best practices. This department then works with people throughout IT by teaching them these best practices and facilitating their IT-wide use.

Your first task is to do some independent research into PMOs in general and the nature of the PMO within your organization. This will expand your PMO knowledge and give you additional data points to help assure that joining a PMO is right for you.

Next, begin your quest by finding out what methodologies and processes are supported by your company's PMO. For example, your company most likely uses an Agile- or Waterfall-based software development methodology. Hopefully you will have the opportunity to learn these supported methodologies as part of your job as a business analyst. If not, learn them on your own.

Your next goal is to gain an understanding of the other processes, methodologies, and software supported by the PMO. Examples of these may include project management software, application documentation standards, and user training processes. Logic would dictate that the PMO should have documentation on these items on the company intranet.

Lastly, if possible, work on projects and cross-department initiatives that include members of the PMO. This will not only allow you to learn exactly what they do, but it will give you a chance to meet them and let them see the quality of your work.

Until next time, work hard, work smart, and continue to grow.

BUILDING YOUR PERSONAL BRAND

Whether you are looking for a job, pushing for a promotion, trying to start your own company, or looking for a date to your sister's wedding, building your personal brand can be of great help. This week's blog can help you with the above three listed professional goals. Regarding your sister's wedding, you're on your own.

Your personal professional brand is your reputation in the workplace. Do people you work with like you? Do they respect you? Do they think you're honest, ethical, hardworking, and so on? A second aspect of your professional brand is your accomplishments and credentials. Let's talk about them both.

You build a quality reputation by trying your best, being helpful, and treating people with respect. From a knowledge and technical perspective, it means being very good at what you do. For example, if you are a Java developer, be the best Java developer you can be. By "best," I don't just mean trying hard. Being your best also means keeping up on the latest technology upgrades, trends, products, vendors, techniques, and methodologies in your professional area. Lastly, it means sharing this knowledge with those you work with. It's this combination of deep knowledge and a willingness to share that transforms you from just a programmer, using the Java example, to a thought leader.

Regarding your professional credentials, they can be categorized in the following ways:

- Business accomplishments
- Educational credentials and certifications
- Industry activism

Your business accomplishments can be accumulated by doing your job well and keeping a list of your successes. In the IT area, this tends to be easier than in professions that are less project oriented. Each time you finish a project, it adds to your accomplishments list. These accomplishments can be put on your resume, used as a stepping-stone to greater responsibility, or even talked about at a party to help you sound interesting and actually get you a date for your sister's wedding. Sorry, just kidding, but it was too good to resist.

Your educational credentials and certifications can be achieved through hard work and a willingness to spend the time and money to learn new things, get that advanced degree, or pass a certification exam. There is no mystery here—it's the time, the money, and a personal situation that allows you to invest your time and money in your future. By the way, this last one is a lot harder than it sounds.

Regarding industry activism, I mean your professional status outside of your job and within your industry. Have you been quoted in ITworld, did you have an article published in *Computerworld*, did you write a book, or were you asked to speak at an important industry conference? If you answered yes to any of these questions, then you are on your way.

Most people think about the first three categories, namely professional reputation, business accomplishments, and educational-/certification-based credentials. All of these items are very important and cannot be overemphasized. Very few people, however, try to grow professionally through industry activism. In addition to great bragging rights in an interview, it can open unexpected doors via the people you meet, the people who read your article, the things you will learn, and other related and unforeseen opportunities.

Until next time, work hard, work smart, and continue to grow.

JOINING IT FROM OTHER PROFESSIONS

As IT insiders, we sometimes forget that there are many people outside of IT in other professions and in other parts of the company that would love to get in. The question "How do I get into IT?" is a question that I have been asked again and again over the years, long before I began writing for ITworld.

Over the years, the nature of our profession has expanded from just techies to include business analysts, testers, web designers, documentation writers, and other nonprogramming and computer-hardware-based positions. As a result, because of the business opportunities, people from other professions such as teaching, accounting, art, and even sales have moved into IT organizations.

The columns included in this chapter are answers to questions received from people in various professions, all generally asking the same question: "Are there any jobs within IT that utilize my skill set?"

My question to you, as people already within the IT ranks, is, do you have other skills not being used within your current job that could/should be showcased as a way to help you move ahead? If you are a Java programmer by day and an artist by night, have you considered bringing them together as a website designer and developer? If you are a business analyst and have a degree in applied mathematics, have you considered working in the financial services industry helping to define and build software that calculates insurance rates or helps pick profitable stocks and bonds? The combinations are endless based on your seemingly non-IT-oriented skills.

Lastly, should you be a tech lead or IT manager and in the position to hire others, you should look at the question "How do I get into IT?" in reverse; in other words, "What nontechnical skill sets are out there that we could take advantage of within IT?" As you read the columns below, think of them from both of these perspectives.

Unlike the other chapters in this book, I'm not going to discuss each column individually because they are all variations of the same theme.

Now, enough for my commentary; enjoy the columns.

GREAT IT JOBS FOR SCIENCE AND MATH MAJORS

The question I was asked:

Even though I have undergraduate degrees in physics and mathematics, I really like computers and would like to work professionally within IT. How can I find a job within IT?

My answer:

Thanks for your e-mail. One of the best ways to get an IT job is by leveraging your knowledge in areas outside of IT. In your case, with a degree in physics, you would be very marketable to IT groups that develop and/or support science-related organizations. This is the case because you have an understanding of the work being performed by the organization you are supporting. In your case, you would be an ideal candidate for IT departments within companies that:

- provide math-related software products/services;
- build products (like airplanes) that require an understanding of physics;
- electronics manufacturers;
- green energy engineering firms;
- other companies in similar industries.

Additional advantages of looking for IT jobs within these industries include:

- you will be marketable to both their internal IT and software engineering departments;
- you will be able to retain and take advantage of some of your physics knowledge;
- it will be easier for you to gain the professional respect of your internal business users because you speak their professional language;
- you will be able to design and develop higher quality software because you have an understanding of science that will be incorporated in the software you will be creating;
- if, at some future point, you decide that IT is not right for you, you can more easily pivot into a business-related role because of your physics and/or math background.

I give you this advice based on my own experience. I personally have two undergraduate degrees, one in accounting and one in computer information systems. Professionally, I always worked within IT, but, because of my accounting background, I always worked on accounting and business-related software applications. My accounting background was of great advantage to me in this role because I had a deep understanding of business fundamentals and processes related to the software I was building. The same should be true for you in the physics and/or mathematics area.

Another thing to consider would be to become an expert in using and supporting specific industry-standard software used in physics and mathematics. The products that first come to mind in this area are MATLAB and Simulink from MathWorks. Gaining an understanding of these products will be much easier for you than someone with a nonscientific background. An understanding of these products can dramatically raise your personal marketability to companies that use them.

As a closing thought, if you truly want to move away from the physics area, your mathematical background can be of great value within the IT groups of financial services firms. There is an enormous amount of mathematics done within insurance firms, asset management firms, and other aspects of the financial industry. In fact, I personally know someone who was trained as a physicist and used his mathematical background to become a portfolio manager specializing in the mathematical analysis of stocks and other investment securities. As you would expect, all of these mathematical analyses are done via specialized software developed via the combined efforts of investment and IT professionals. My point here is not that the financial services industry is right for you. My point is that your knowledge and understanding of physics and mathematics is very transferable into a number of other industries.

Until next time, work hard, work smart, and continue to grow.

CHANGING CAREER FROM FINANCE TO IT

The question I was asked:

I went to school for accounting and have worked in the finance department of my company for about three years. During this time, I have worked closely with the IT department on installing a new general ledger, accounts receivable, and accounts payable system. Through this experience, I learned I have a love for technology and would like to move into an IT-related job. How can I do this with no formal IT training or computer programming experience?

My answer:

To begin, congratulations on the implementation of your new financial systems. You didn't specifically say in your question that the implementation went well, but by saying you have developed a love for technology, I'm assuming it did. :)

There are a number of great jobs within IT that do not require the ability to program. These jobs include business analyst, software tester, project manager, application trainer, documentation writer, and web designer. Please note that there are also a number of job types in the helpdesk, hardware, and data center areas, but given you are coming from finance, I'm assuming you do not have the background or interest in these types of positions.

The best way to transition into a job within IT is to find a position that takes advantage of your existing skills, knowledge, and experience. For example, as a finance person you have a strong understanding of accounting and potentially other activities performed within the finance function. These activities could include budgeting, cash management, product line profitability analysis, revenue projections, etc. Look for a job within IT where this knowledge would be valuable. For example, the role of business analyst is generally responsible for defining software business requirements and enhancements. You would be ideal for this on a finance-related project because of your deep understanding of the business area. This would also be true for testing, training, and/or documentation type roles.

Lastly, if you are serious about moving into IT as your profession, I would strongly suggest taking a beginner's programming class in Java, .NET, or other mainstream programming technology. I'm not suggesting you become a professional programmer, but as an IT professional, it would be advantageous for you to know what programming is and how it works. This knowledge will allow you to work more closely with the programming staff and better position you for more senior IT roles.

Until next time, work hard, work smart, and continue to grow.

SOME GREAT IT JOBS FOR ENGLISH MAJORS

The question I was asked:

I graduated from college last year with a degree in English and have not been able to find a job. I have always liked and been comfortable using computers. Are there jobs in IT that combine my interest in computers and my degree in English?

My answer:

In short, yes, there are a number of jobs within IT where writing ability is greatly valued. I'll begin by listing the job types, then give you couple of examples, and end with a short description of each job. These jobs are: social media consultant, web designer, documentation writer, training materials development, and business analyst.

I have a friend with a strong writing background and a degree in marketing. He also liked technology and wanted to move toward a position within IT. He jokingly insists that the social media industry was created specifically to give him this opportunity. He invested some time into learning the ins and outs of various business-oriented social media tools, such as Twitter, HootSuite, WordPress, and a few other products. Then, he found a job within an IT group helping the marketing department implement the company's social media/marketing program. He is now the manager of social media systems within the IT organization and is dotted line to the VP of marketing.

As a second example, I once had a great business analyst working for me. She went to school for journalism but also had a fascination for all things technical. Because of her journalism background, she had an incredible ability to interview business users and properly document their conversations. As a result, she was able to draft great business requirements documents.

As promised above, here are short descriptions of the various IT positions listed above:

1. **Social media consultant**: Works specifically on social media and active listening type software/systems.

2. **Web designer and copy writer**: Works on the design, structure, and textual content on company websites.

3. **Documentation writer**: Writes internal documentation on systems, processes, and other IT-related activities.

4. **Training materials developer**: Writes training material to be used as a part of rolling out new software applications

5. **Business analyst**: Works with users to define the business requirements for IT-related projects, including software purchase, new software development, and existing software enhancements.

Until next time, work hard, work smart, and continue to grow.

FIVE GREAT IT JOBS FOR ARTISTS

The question I was asked:

I'm currently unemployed and want to make a career change into IT. I'm also an amateur but accomplished painter and photographer and enjoy making home movies of my family. I like using technology, but I am not well schooled on the topic. What would you suggest?

My answer:

The combination of heavy artistic ability and light technical skill can be extremely profitable. To make it so, however, you will need to expand your technology background based on which of the following jobs sounds most interesting to you. As you will see, these are all great potential jobs, but require different types of technical skills.

Website designer

Web designers, as the title implies, design the look, feel, and flow of websites. For you to perform this job correctly, given your artistic background, the use of color and visual design would most likely be very natural to you. The key things you would need to learn would be:

- An understanding of website navigation best practices;
- Ideally, a working knowledge of HTML. This would allow you to design web pages in their native format as well as

gain an appreciation of what is easy and hard to technically create.
- A strong working knowledge of Photoshop and/or other graphical-related software.
- An appreciation for web development. I am by no means suggesting that you learn to do it, but having an understanding of the processes and challenges will allow you to better design websites that are both functional to use and cost effective to build.

Video designer and producer

Videos have become the gold standard in web-based marketing, e-learning, website enhancement, web-based advertising, and other similar online activities. That said, professional speakers, advertising agencies, training companies, web design firms, and other businesses are all using in-house and/or contracted videographers to produce web-based content. Given your interest and presumed ability in making quality movies, the hurdle for you is to develop a working knowledge of industry-standard video editing software for both Apple and PC type computers. Also, if you want to do freelance in this area, you will most likely need your own video camera and lighting equipment.

Flash automation designer

Flash is like a video and, in some cases, is simply converted video content. It may, however, also be created using a number of other tools, technologies, and processes. For example, my company's IT management training company uses the advanced automation features in Microsoft PowerPoint to create our e-learning materials and then uses iSpring Presenter to convert it to flash. There are also a number of other great tools by Adobe and other software vendors that you can use in the Flash creation process.

Green screen production designer

This is a technology/process that is continuing to gain popularity. It's basically using the same technology that is used on TV to give the weather report. This technology is being used more and more in everything from web-based training materials to the advertisements you see pop up on your computer when you visit various websites. To do green screen work properly, you need an understanding of video production (described earlier), lighting, and the software needed to blend captured video with the desired green screen background (which may also be video). From a technology perspective, there are various industry-standard technologies available on both Apple and PC computers that allow you, with a little practice, to fairly easily create green screen productions. Also, if you want to do freelance in this area, you will most likely need your own green screen (generally lime-green-colored cloth), video camera, and lighting equipment, and a place to produce it.

Data visualization

This potential job option is very different than those previously described. This job, as the name implies, is the process of presenting data in graphical ways that help make data easily intelligible. This includes the use of standard data presentation vehicles, such as pie charts and line and bar graphs. At first glance, this may seem rather simplistic, but to do it right is truly an art form. The reason is threefold:

- First, pie charts and simple bar graphs are not your only options. There are an enormous number of 2D and 3D graphical paradigms that can be used, both singularly and in combination.
- Second, to perform this task effectively, you should have a strong understanding of data. In fact, a background in statistics would also be of value.

- Third, you would need the technical ability to create these visual data representations using Microsoft Excel and potentially any one of a number of advanced graphical software packages.

Until next time, work hard, work smart, and continue to grow.

FINAL THOUGHTS

I hope that you have found this book to be of value and have gained insights that will help you today and throughout your career.

Writing a book of this type is a funny thing. Because it is primarily a collection of previously published columns, I felt I had a strong sense, before beginning its compilation, of which topics would most likely be of highest value to those who read the book. That said, my first step in the book's creation was to reread my year's worth of columns. Upon doing so, I realized that I was incorrect. It was true that I knew how many people read each column and that I had an understanding of all the comments, good, bad, and indifferent, that were written about my topics, but what I realized is that all of the included topics were of interest to some of my readership. About half of the columns were directly inspired by reader questions, many others were based on face-to-face conversations I had with techies at various venues, and a few were conceived in my own head based on my understanding of current IT industry trends and my own professional experiences.

My hope for you, having presumably just read the book in its entirely and found it of appropriate value to make it all the way to the book's ending thoughts, is that some of the topics, insights, suggestions, and advice given within this book resonated with you personally and provided helpful takeaways for today and throughout your career.

One more interesting thing about writing a book that is a collection of ongoing smaller works is that the work continues after the book is published. At the time of this printing I have already written many of the columns for my next book. These columns, listed in publication order, are:

- "Power of the business analyst/project manager combo"
- "Fifteen tips on how to write your resume like it's a marketing brochure"
- "Ten questions that can help you be more innovative at work"
- "Seven ways to talk with business users"
- "Stay technical or become a manager: ten things to consider"
- "Ten ways using Skype can help you professionally"
- "Looking for a job outside your industry"
- "Two very hard, but doable, steps to becoming a technical thought leader"
- "Having a prestigious company on your resume has value"
- "Twelve tips when writing e-mails and business communication"
- "Fifteen tips to maximize your home office productivity (part 1)"
- "Fifteen ways to maximize your home office productivity (part 2)"
- "How entrepreneurship can help your job search—a real life example"
- "Ten ways to maintain your professional connections"
- "When job searching, time is not your friend"
- "Five steps to revitalize your IT skill set"
- "Three steps to get the best projects to work on"
- "Six ways to start thinking like a CIO, and how they can help you get there"

- "Being a specialist or generalist: a techie's dilemma"
- "Importance of resume and social media consistency"
- "Soft skills on a techie's resume: you must be kidding"
- "How to add soft skills to your resume"
- "Five reasons teaching technology to others is good for you"

If you don't want to wait for my next book to read these columns, they can be found on the ITworld website at http://www.itworld.com/blogs/eric-bloom.

As a final thought and request, if there is a topic you wish I had written about or a question you have regarding your IT career, please let me know. If I have the knowledge and/or can do the research, I'll try to write on your required topic. Truth be told, I would love your input. As I said in the acknowledgments, my column readers make the writing worthwhile.

Lastly, and in closing this book, I have learned through my professional career that a profession is truly a journey, not a destination. Each time I attained a professional goal, got the promotion I really wanted, was laid off, learned that latest technology, was disappointed with a turn of events, or was recognized for a specific achievement, the pain or pleasure was short-lived, and I marched forward. I know this personal philosophy is not for all. I have met many very successful people at all organizational levels and professional vocations who truly love exactly what they are doing and want to do throughout the remainder of their careers. If you are someone like me, enjoy the journey. If you are not, enjoy and cherish the destination. In both cases, or if you are somewhere in between, I wish you happiness and professional satisfaction.

Until next time, work hard, work smart, and continue to grow.

Best wishes,

Eric

www.ingramcontent.com/pod-product-compliance
Lightning Source LLC
Chambersburg PA
CBHW061505180526
45171CB00001B/43